The Humane Home

The
HUMANE
HOME

Easy Steps for Sustainable & Green Living

Sarah Lozanova

ILLUSTRATIONS BY CANDACE ROSE RARDON

Princeton Architectural Press · New York

Published by
Princeton Architectural Press
202 Warren Street
Hudson, New York 12534
www.papress.com

ISBN 978-1-61689-850-2

Editor: Kristen Hewitt
Designer: Paul Wagner
Design assistance: Paula Baver
Illustrations: Candace Rose Rardon

Library of Congress Control Number:
2020946804

MIX
Paper from
responsible sources
FSC
www.fsc.org   FSC® C104723

INTRODUCTION
What Is the Humane Home? 7

INTRODUCTION
What Is the Humane Home?

D EVELOPING YOUR OWN VISION of a sustainable home is a personal journey that involves exploring your values and lifestyle choices. When thinking about sustainable living, homesteading often comes to mind. While not practical for everyone, it can afford opportunities for self-sufficiency and connection to the natural world. But there are many other ways to create a green life: One vision might involve renting an apartment near public transportation lines, supporting local farmers' markets, and joining a community solar farm to source electricity. Another might include building a modest and highly efficient house, using native plants in the yard to attract wildlife, and limiting purchases.

This book is designed to inspire each of us to take action, wherever we call home. Each chapter examines a different aspect of living: Deciding where to live and the type of home we occupy sets the stage. How we heat, cool, and power our homes impacts the quantity and type of energy we use. The food we consume impacts land use, the local economy, and waste generation. Landscaping approaches and techniques shape the natural world around our homes and beyond. Mindful water use helps protect our most valuable resource. We make our home air healthy by only bringing in safe products, avoiding mold growth, and ventilating properly.

Follow your passion, whether you are interested in making your yard into an oasis for wildlife, starting an herb garden on the patio, or reducing your utility bills. Discover which chapters resonate most with you and inspire you to act. Which project ideas seem fun? Including children, friends, or family can add momentum and joy to the process. Use each accomplishment to help inspire new actions.

Start composting food waste and then start a vegetable garden with the resulting soil enrichment. Install low-flow showerheads and then see if there is a difference in your energy bills or water use. Make your own personal essential oil blends with some friends, and give your favorites away as homemade gifts. Experiment and create your unique version of the humane home.

Ultimately, the humane home is about reinventing our relationship with nature, our belongings, our food systems, our neighbors, and our communities. Let's cherish and celebrate this opportunity.

ONE

ESTABLISHING YOUR HUMANE HOME

Enjoy Voluntary
Simplicity

W HETHER WE LIVE IN A house or an apartment, alone
or with others, our homes allow for embracing our
lives. Aligning our homes with our values and aspira-
tions sets the stage for embracing sustainability and living in a way
that is in harmony with nature. In deciding how and where we want
to live, we can work to simplify our lives and reduce our material
needs, find ways to be in community with others, embrace transportation modes that reduce carbon emissions, and create mindful
living spaces where we can live out these intentions.

What brings the most meaning to your life? For many people,
the answer is relationships, health, security, or a sense of purpose.
Focusing on material goals can be an obstacle to achieving this, as it
results in investing more energy into supporting expensive homes,
cars, and other belongings rather than in putting effort toward the
real priorities.

Voluntary simplicity, a term popularized by Duane Elgin, is
a lifestyle that focuses on core values instead of consumerism and
material possessions. It embraces simple pleasures and conscious

consumption, recognizing that we can still live very well while having less. By slowing the pace of living and focusing on core values, it's possible to have more time and freedom to pursue what is most important and rewarding, whether making home-cooked meals from scratch, purchasing durable goods, spending time outdoors, nourishing social connections, learning, or exploring.

To make a shift toward voluntary simplicity, it is important to identify the elements of your life that are unmanageable or overly complicated. Large homes, long commutes, high bills, unfulfilling relationships or jobs, and too many commitments are some of the common culprits. Voluntary simplicity involves reorienting life away from consumerism and toward fulfillment and redefining relationships to money, consumption, possessions, the earth, and one another.

Once a certain level of material comfort is met, as studies have found, increasing our wealth and the number of possessions does not further happiness. In fact, it may hinder contentment if it creates a sense of entrapment in our chosen lifestyles. For example, buying a new car can result in high monthly payments that drain resources from other areas of life. If you're able to manage it, lowering your expenses can allow you to take on a less demanding job or work fewer hours, allowing you to spend more time with family and friends and to pursue your passions.

Downsizing and Decluttering

One of the easiest ways to begin a lifestyle that embraces voluntary simplicity is to downsize. Bigger living quarters have higher energy usage, higher taxes, and larger insurance bills; they require more upkeep and cleaning and have more furniture and appliances. There is also a good deal more space to fill, encouraging more purchases and

more stuff. Living in a large home might be worth it for some people who truly value entertaining, or for large households who can take full advantage of the space. For most of us, though, the demands of maintaining a large house needlessly consume energy and resources from other parts of life.

Moving to a smaller, less expensive residence can be a great way to simplify life and regain time and money. Other examples include giving up an extra vehicle, taking vacations closer to home, and reducing discretionary spending. By donating unneeded possessions you can help others in need.

Each of us can benefit and learn from examining where down-sizing is possible in our lives without hindering our quality of life. Smaller, less expensive cars typically use less gas and have lower sticker prices and insurance costs. Examine which possessions are necessary or truly bring joy and which create clutter. It is easy to collect extraneous books, kitchen gadgets, music, clothing, decorations, and memorabilia that are rarely used yet take up space and consume mental energy. Some friendships or volunteer commitments may also drain our inner resources yet fail to align with realizing an inspired life.

Our living spaces shape how we spend our time in them through their layouts, contents, and infrastructures. Our homes not only reflect us but also are the containers for our home lives. Setting up our living space with a vision of how we want to live in mind can help manifest it.

Using natural materials helps create a calm environment. Removing clutter and maintaining open spaces can spur creativity and uplifting ideas. Utilizing natural light and indoor plants can invigorate and boost mood and productivity. Allowing easy access to the outdoors encourages venturing out, exploring, and harvesting.

To gain a greater alliance with the outside world and familiarity with the wildlife in the yard, locate seating areas strategically to take in the view. Placing bird feeders near the window is a great way to encourage a connection with our feathered friends. Be conscious of how window treatments, although effective at insulating against extreme temperatures, can also obscure our views of the outdoors.

Be mindful of how you use technology in your home. As valuable as technology can be as a tool, it can also be a major distraction. Give thought to where you keep computers and TV screens. Consider keeping dining areas screen-free so that everyone can focus on, and appreciate, the food and each other's company.

Consider what activities you most want to do in your home and create versatile spaces in which to complete these activities. If you want to socialize with close friends, create comfortable spaces that promote lively conversations. To cook healthy meals, have high-quality food, sauces, oils, and spices on hand, along with the needed kitchen equipment. If you want to make handcrafts, design a space for creative endeavors. To increase mindfulness, carve out an area to meditate, do yoga, or practice tai chi. If you value reading, create a cozy nook with good lighting. If and when you are no longer interested in a hobby or activity, give away or sell the associated materials to open up space for something new.

LEARN MORE: Consider a Tiny House

The average person in the United States spends 37 percent of their income on housing. Most of us spend about seven or so hours a day sleeping and often about the same time, or more, working or out and about, meaning we spend *a lot* on housing, considering how little time we spend awake at home.

One way to drastically reduce housing costs is to go small, very small. The tiny house movement is gaining momentum as more people rethink their priorities. For some, this involves creating a miniature dream home. Not only can they cost less, but they have a much smaller carbon footprint than a traditional home.

What Is a Tiny House?

Most tiny homes are between one hundred and four hundred square feet and are meant for year-round living. This architectural and social movement considers how much space we really need to be comfortable and happy. In some cases, the reduction in living costs allows for early retirement or greater financial freedom.

They can come in all shapes, from the traditional "house" design to yurts and repurposed shipping containers. They are planned to use every square inch of space as efficiently as possible. Tiny houses are typically insulated and often customized and have a durable construction.

Similar to typical houses, they contain a kitchen, a sleeping space, a living area, and storage, but they are trimmed down to a much smaller size. In many cases, the appliances and utilities, including space heaters, water heaters, stoves, and toilets, are designed for boats and RVs and translate well to a tiny house setting.

Storage space is often carved out in little nooks. Certain areas of the home serve multiple purposes, depending on the need. Outside areas are maximized, making it easier to enjoy the outdoors and entertain.

Many people design and even build their own tiny house. Some have a ground foundation while others are on wheels. Some are prefabricated while others are built from scratch, possibly with repurposed materials. Increasingly, architects and builders are specializing in this niche market.

Adjusting to a Smaller Way of Life

Embracing and enjoying life in a tiny house involves significant downsizing for most and requires purging unused or unneeded possessions, from kitchenware, clothing, and personal care products to office supplies, books and magazines, hobby materials, furniture, and linens. Digitizing mail, files, books, photographs, and music collections can help.

Tiny living requires redefining our relationship to things—this is often easier said than done. It is a good idea to have a test run to determine if tiny living is a good fit for you. A less dramatic alternative to a tiny house is simply a small house, less than one thousand square feet.

Pros and Cons of Living in a Tiny House

Smaller houses are easier to clean and require less energy to operate. They have lower property taxes and insurance premiums. Many people are able to build them without a mortgage or are able to pay off the debt quickly, resulting in greater financial freedom. In other cases, the cost is similar to a larger home because it contains custom-designed features and high-end materials.

It is important to consult local building codes to determine if a structure meets legal regulations. For example, some tiny homes with a foundation are smaller than the minimum required square footage. Houses on wheels may be considered RVs, which might not be allowed outside of an RV park. For a tiny house to be towed to a new location without a special permit, it needs to fit a specific maximum size requirement.

The State of Oregon has amended building codes to allow sleeping lofts and alternative stairs, benefitting the tiny house movement, all thanks to the work of tiny house advocates supporting policy changes. Their goal is to make tiny houses a mainstream housing option. These ingenious structures can help mitigate the affordable-housing crisis and spur economic development.

Find Your Community

"Man is by nature a social creature."
—Aristotle

J OINING A COMMUNITY CAN PROVIDE strength, inspiration, and rich resources, whether in the form of ideas, connections, or support. The ties that forge a community can vary—some are based on shared activities or learning, on service, on religion or spiritual practice, or simply on a more social and community-oriented approach to life.

Your home and living situation can be a great opportunity to create connections with others, whether with roommates, neighbors, or the extended family. More commonly, people—and not just young people—are choosing to live with others who are not a part of their immediate families, finding it to be more supportive, sustainable, and fun. There are many approaches to living with others, and choosing what's right for you depends on what kind of lifestyle you want.

Consider Communal Living

Communal living can take many different forms, including an informal arrangement of sharing a house and living expenses with friends or members of one's extended family. There are also cooperative houses that have a structured approach, such as leases for individual bedrooms and requirements for contributing to housework. Some communities involve renting while others are primarily owner occupied. Cohousing is a collaborative neighborhood in which residents have private homes with a bathroom and kitchen and actively participate in its design and operation.

Some communities serve a specific population, such as senior citizens or college students. Others are multigenerational and have members from many walks of life. Some are located on small urban lots; others have many acres in rural areas. If you enjoy being surrounded by others, communal or multigenerational living can offer many benefits, from shared meals and chores to reduced living expenses.

Embracing a sense of community also doesn't necessarily have to involve living together. It could include engaging in neighborhood potlucks, skill-building workshops, musical events, or sharing childcare. Some communities organize a meal train when somebody is ill or share a collective toolshed or garden plots. Roommates can also add elements of cooperation into an existing living situation by enjoying meals together, carpooling, or splitting chores.

Living in community, whatever the type, can help us to remain open to people from a variety of backgrounds and life experiences. It also allows us to learn from others and strive for a deep understanding of the world around us.

PROFILE: Cohousing at Ithaca Ecovillage

It's the mission statement of Ithaca Ecovillage to promote experiential learning about ways of meeting human needs for shelter, food, energy, livelihood, and social connectedness that are aligned with the long-term health and viability of Earth and all its inhabitants.

Ithaca Ecovillage, in the Finger Lakes region of Upstate New York, is the largest cohousing community in the world. With one hundred houses on 175 acres, this multigenerational community houses approximately one hundred fifty adults and sixty children. Ithaca Ecovillage has an organic community-supported agriculture (CSA) vegetable and fruit farm, a pick-your-own berry farm, and a teaching farm for new farmers. The community property also features meadows, ponds, woodlands, a sauna, and basketball courts.

The homes are clustered to preserve green spaces and encourage social interaction. This layout stands in contrast to most new neighborhoods in the US that are automobile-centered, which significantly reduces contact with neighbors. The community is divided into three neighborhoods, each with a distinct character and containing thirty to forty dwellings. Every house incorporates a passive solar design with large south-facing windows and lots of insulation. Many homes have three 50 kW solar arrays in addition to solar hot water and solar electric systems.

The apartments and houses in the newest of the three neighborhoods were built between 2012 and 2015 and are between 440 and 1,440 square feet. All homes are built to the Passive House standard, a rigorous and voluntary set of energy-efficient building requirements. In the newest neighborhood, the dwellings use up to 75 percent less energy for heating and cooling than an average new residence.

Optional shared dinners and social gatherings in the neighborhood common houses and impromptu interactions reduce the need to drive to social gatherings and add a richness to daily life. The community has a shared woodshop, lawnmowers, a tractor, workout room, and swimming ponds. By design, the community makes informally sharing tools, bikes, childcare, meal preparation, and even cars very simple.

A community common house contains fifteen apartments and shared spaces, including guest bedrooms, a large dining room, a kitchen, and a children's playroom available to all neighborhood residents. The common spaces offset the smaller-than usual size of the individual homes by providing a setting for entertaining large groups, attending yoga classes, hosting overnight guests, playing with children, making music, and storing food in the root cellar. Cohousing is an excellent alternative to traditional living that offers high standards with fewer resources.

Cohousing has become a global movement of people seeking to live comfortably and in a community while also contributing to the planet's social, environmental, and economic well-being. A common mission and shared values help unite the community.

Opt for Clean Transportation

C ARS HAVE GIVEN US FREEDOM and the luxury of spreading out—but at a very high cost. Urban sprawl, the loss of farmland and wildlife habitat, air pollution, and carbon emissions are all unfortunate by-products of a car-dependent society. But there are many ways to reduce the amount we drive.

Drive Less, Walk More

Walking or biking is a great way to explore your neighborhood and get to know the people, locally owned businesses, and parks in the area. In addition to saving gas, walking is a great way to stay active.

Take Public Transit

In many cities, public transportation is efficient, affordable, and simple. It helps reduce traffic congestion and can free up time for reading or other simple bus- and train-friendly activities. Long-distance buses and trains are also a great way to reduce air travel, which consumes a large amount of fuel and is a significant contributor of emissions.

Drive an Energy-Efficient Vehicle

Hybrid cars are especially efficient in improving gas mileage for city driving and can reduce overall emissions. Unfortunately, they also employ lithium-ion batteries that have associated environmental issues.

The range of electric vehicles has increased dramatically in recent years, making them an appealing option. When running on renewable energy, electric vehicles are a cleaner alternative to traditional gas-powered vehicles. (This is not necessarily the case when coal-powered electricity is used to charge the vehicle.) Electricity typically costs less than gasoline, making electric vehicles cheaper to operate. Furthermore, electric vehicles require less maintenance than vehicles with internal combustion engines and are cheaper to service.

There are also many fuel-efficient, nonhybrid or nonelectric cars that are modestly priced. (You can find information through Consumer Reports and the EPA's FuelEconomy.gov website.)

Get Rid of Your Car

If you are able to get around without a private car or use it very sparingly, consider giving it up entirely or reducing the number of cars in your household. You can replace with a combination of walking, biking, public transit, and carpooling, and you will save not only on car payments but also on your insurance bill, gas, and repairs.

Live in a Walkable Community

Most urbanites have much better access to public transportation than their rural counterparts. When you are deciding where to live, walkability, bikeability, and public transportation are key considerations in shifting away from a car-centered lifestyle. The easier it is to join the clean-transportation movement, the more it will become part of daily life.

Advocate for Change

Many urban planners are conscious of the problems of sprawl, and there are movements to protect farmland and wildlife habitat, creating greenways around cities. Improved public-transportation systems in some areas shorten commutes and reduce traffic congestion. People and pedal-powered commutes are growing in popularity. There are many ways to participate in these movements. Advocating with your public officials and representatives for reliable and affordable public transit, walking trails, and bike lanes can help propel the momentum.

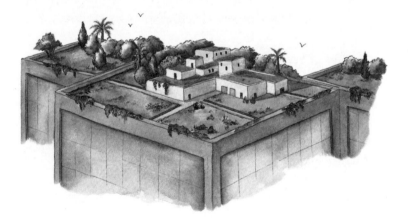

Borrow Locally to Sustainably Finance Your Home

F OR MANY HOMEOWNERS, a mortgage is their largest monthly expense. Taking out a mortgage through a local bank or credit union rather than a large commercial bank can be a great way of supporting and sustaining your community. Plus, credit unions often can offer lower interest rates on mortgages.

Credit unions are nonprofit and community owned and operated. They are generally cooperative institutions that keep money invested within a community with home buyers and local businesses, and often make local investments in sustainability. Borrowing through a credit union creates a symbiotic relationship between lender, borrower, and the larger community.

Borrowing locally is also a good idea if you are seeking a loan for an alternative sustainable building project. It can be difficult for banks to understand projects that stray from the mainstream: for instance, the shared common spaces or unique parking layouts of cohousing communities might lead a national bank to reject a loan. Local banks are more likely to understand the specifics of your project and to be more flexible and open-minded about offering a loan.

LEARN MORE: Working from Home

The coronavirus pandemic of 2020 created turmoil around the world. It also caused many of us to spend more time at home than ever before. One of the rare benefits of the crisis was decreased emissions in some areas. Air quality in many places temporarily improved as planes were grounded and factories closed down. Perhaps a lesson to be learned from this difficult situation is how to reduce carbon emissions and air pollution by working more effectively from home.

Working from home certainly has its perks. You can work in your pajamas and hang out with your dog all day. You can save a lot of gas and money because there is no commute.

Unfortunately, many people really struggle with it. A major reason is that many of the habits we have at home do not support productivity. Working from home suddenly requires us to be disciplined instead of relaxing—or sleeping, recreating, cooking, or cleaning—and for families with children at home, the situation is even trickier to navigate. To better cope with the distractions and temptations of working from home, create an intentional workspace that supports concentration and focus.

Clear the Clutter

Make sure your space is organized (especially if it is small)—this will help keep you focused on your priorities. Clutter can also cause stress—keep your space clear so you want to spend time there. If you find your productivity dipping, organizing or tidying your workspace can give you a boost.

Carve Out a Work Spot

If you don't have a dedicated office or spare bedroom with a door, consider whether there is a nook or corner you can take over as a workspace in your home. This might involve setting up a desk or table in a quiet area of your apartment. However small, being in a designated workspace signals that you are ready to focus on work.

Create a Daily Routine

Designate work hours and set an alarm to keep yourself on track. Many of us have a routine around going into the office. With that in mind, create a similar routine for beginning your working-at-home day. If you started your day by showering, eating breakfast, and making coffee before going into the office, engage in a similar routine before you go to your workspace. This routine signals that your day is ready to start and will help you shift into work mode.

Set Boundaries with Your Time

Make a work schedule and stick to it. Schedules that are acceptable or unacceptable at the office will also likely be similarly acceptable at home. For example, silence your cell phone unless you need to be available for emergencies or you need it for work. Only check your personal email or social media platforms if you are on a dedicated break. Likewise, when your workday is done, do something else. Shutting off your computer or leaving your designated workspace are great ways of setting a boundary between work time and personal time.

Take Advantage of Being at Home

Keep your fridge full of healthy foods to curb unhealthy snacking and to make energizing lunches during the workday. Find practices that really help you to refresh and recharge throughout the day—use your bike for an errand, go for a walk in your neighborhood, meditate, stretch, or even take a short power nap.

TWO

SUSTAINABLE BUILDING MATERIALS AND TECHNIQUES

Use Sustainable Building Materials and Practices

≈

I N NATURE, THERE IS ALMOST NO WASTE. Unneeded materials from one process become vital contributions to another. Ultimately, the way we build and maintain our homes needs to more fundamentally align with the way ecosystems work. Whether you are building a new home or doing a renovation or smaller home improvement project, there are an array of sustainable building methods and practices available, from using modern eco-friendly building materials to repurposing construction waste to exploring earthen building or other traditional building techniques. Building with sustainable materials and practices not only has a positive impact on the environment but on our health and quality of life.

What brings the most meaning to your life? For many people, the answer is relationships, health, security, or a sense of purpose. Focusing on material goals can be an obstacle to achieving this, as it results in investing more energy into supporting expensive homes, cars, and other belongings rather than in putting effort toward the real priorities.

In the United States, Europe, and most industrialized countries, home construction consumes a large quantity of resources. Many construction products are imported from Asia, producing gas emissions in long-distance transport. While we give thought to the impacts of heating, cooling, and powering a home, it is equally important to consider the carbon footprint and ecological impact of the materials that go into the house itself, even for simple remodeling projects. Sourcing building materials from close to home supports the local economy and reduces transport emissions; it can also ensure that the materials were produced in safe working conditions with nontoxic ingredients.

Avoid Common Contaminants

The building products found in our homes shape our air quality and dictate our chemical exposure. Sadly, many building products are a toxic soup of harmful ingredients. This is exacerbated in houses without adequate ventilation (see page 145).

Formaldehyde, known to cause certain types of cancer, is commonly found in flooring, cabinetry, plywood, insulation, glues, and adhesives. Acetaldehyde, another carcinogen and respiratory irritant, is found in laminate, cork, and linoleum products. Methylene chloride, a toxin commonly found in adhesives, can cause respiratory issues and fatigue.

Whenever possible, seek products that do not contain harmful chemicals. Look for Green Seal–certified products, which meet higher standards for health and sustainability.

Choose Green Building Professionals

When building an eco-friendly home, it is essential to find architects and builders with experience in sourcing local and natural materials and in resource-saving practices. For example, accreditation with LEED and Passive House guarantees that they have some knowledge of eco-friendly features.

Find Regional Manufacturers

Determining what locally produced building materials are available for windows, doors, insulation, cement, siding, roofing, flooring, wood products, counters, and plumbing fixtures is a great way to learn about local building distributors and about if and why their products are healthier for and friendly to the environment.

Natural and Earthen
Building Traditions

I N NEARLY EVERY LOCALE, nature provides building materials. Look around at the landscape to get ideas for locally appropriate supplies. Bamboo is one of the fastest-growing plants on the earth and has numerous uses as a construction material in many regions. Rocks, soil, straw, sand, wood, and plant-based pigments are excellent choices in many areas, especially when they are locally harvested. What wood products are sustainably harvested and milled in your area? Is locally mined granite available?

In the highlands of the Andes Mountains, there are small villages with structures constructed exclusively of adobe. The homes have thatched roofs, and the yards are partitioned with simple stick fences. If the soil is red, so are the exterior walls of the houses. If trees are sparse in number, rocks are used to create fences. The communities are an extension of the landscape and are made up of the same natural elements. At the end of the house's life, most of its elements become pieces of a giant compost pile and are returned to the earth.

In the Great Plains of the United States, many European settlers created sod houses in the 1800s and early 1900s because they lacked access to wood and stone. In Nebraska, settlers sought out fields of buffalo grass, wire grass, little bluestem, prairie cordgrass, Indian grass, and wheatgrass. These grasses have densely packed roots that hold the soil together. The sod was cut into bricks to construct homes with walls that were about two feet thick.

Although you may not choose to live in a rustic sod structure, the use of earthen building materials can be adapted to a given locale and the end results can be beautiful and clean in feeling. Natural clay plasters can beautify the interior of a home and can be created from local soils in many areas. Straw can be baled and stacked to create insulated exterior walls. Rammed earth walls can be created from gravel, sand, silt, and clay. Cobb homes are made from a mixture of clay, sand, and straw.

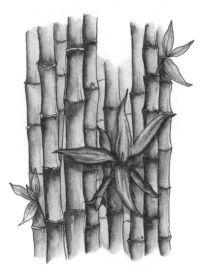

PROFILE: Modern Earthen Floors:
Reviving an Ancient Technique

Earthen floors have been around for millennia and are still used in much of the world. Modern earthen floors are very different from dirt floors that release dust into the air. Each one is unique and handcrafted, telling its own story. Whereas dirt floors are unsealed, modern earthen floors are made of tempered-down layers. They are then treated with linseed oil, making them firm and water-repellent.

These floors have roots in the homes of the native southwest of the United States—the tradition passed down for generations until the trade was nearly lost as modern building techniques were adopted. Sukita Raey, a natural builder in Portland, Oregon, has been installing earthen floors for two decades. Their subtle beauty, the way they feel underfoot, and their texture enthrall her: "Earthen floors are wonderful to walk on. That's an amazing thing to say about a floor." She finds many people drawn to them, but so few people know how to make them.

Each year, Raey leads workshops to teach others how to create these floors in their own homes. Many of her students have gone on to successfully install earthen floors of their own, keeping the tradition and the craft alive. The technique is relatively easy to learn for someone handy and accustomed to DIY projects.

For new homes, Raey adds several inches of drainage rocks down to create a subfloor. Next, she puts a vapor barrier down to prevent moisture from moving up through the floor system. Then she adds several inches of insulation, like pumice or rigid foam, topped by several inches of tempered road base. After that, she puts down an earthen finish of sand, clay, and straw. Finally, Raey treats floors with several coats of high-quality, premium linseed oil.

Raey estimates that most earthen floors cost about $5.50 per square foot when using quality oil and free labor. She recommends using premium oils so that the floors last decades and also sanding and resealing them every five to ten years. In many cases, on-site materials can be used with minimum processing.

In addition to their beauty, these floors also have impressive environmental attributes. According to Raey, they have the least amount of embodied carbon of any flooring because they require the least processing. The carbon footprint of building materials has been under greater scrutiny lately as understanding increases about the preconstruction impact of construction materials.

Because they are easy to clean and don't off-gas when natural oils are applied, earthen floors also promote clean indoor air. Raey sweeps, mops, and uses an oil-based soap to clean her floors. She takes pride in her work and enjoys watching them stand the test of time.

Reclaim Materials and Repurpose Waste

W HEN YOU THINK ABOUT LANDFILLS, do you think of rotting disposable diapers, discarded carrots, and unfashionable clothing? In truth, a large portion of the material in landfills is waste from building and road construction. In 2015, the United States generated 548 million tons of construction and demolition debris, more than twice the amount of municipal solid waste (which includes household, office, and retail waste).

Many of the building materials we throw away can be reused and repurposed, whether in home construction, remodeling, or landscaping. Homes that use recycled materials are one of a kind and have character. Using salvaged materials can also save money and conserve resources, but it requires a lot of planning and a willingness to be flexible and creative.

Customize a Home of Reclaimed Materials

When constructing or remodeling a house, it often needs to be tailored to the climate and the materials at hand. One approach is to determine what salvaged materials are available and then to plan the design accordingly. Another approach is to design the residence and then collect the needed reclaimed materials. Either way, lots of time, determination, and storage space will be helpful.

Use Recycled Materials

Wood beams and ceramic tile can be reclaimed from older homes. Bottles can be placed in earthen or mortar walls to allow light to shine through the colored glass. Bricks can be recovered from construction rubble and cleaned to make beautiful features, including patios, brick ovens, and pathways. One-trip shipping containers can be converted into storage sheds or guest rooms or combined with others to make more complex structures. Concrete can be crushed and used as aggregate for walkways and driveways. Sinks, vanities, bathtubs, cabinets, shower stalls, and even toilets can be repurposed.

There are also many construction materials on the market made from recycled materials. Just a few examples you might find are: composite lumber and bricks made from plastic bottles, tile and countertops made from recycled glass, cellulose insulation made from old newspapers, and flooring and panels made from cork bottle stoppers.

How to Find Salvaged Materials

One of the easiest ways to reclaim materials is to visit demolition sites. Be sure to secure permission from the contractor before removing materials. If you are looking for something in particular, let them know, and they might be willing to set materials aside.

Construction sites are another good source of waste in the form of surplus or slightly damaged materials. Again, before removing materials, ask the foreman for permission and guidance. Antique malls, architectural salvage stores, and home improvement donation centers are good sources of anything from windows and doors to hardware, tile, and plumbing.

Some people have also purchased properties with material reuse in mind. Old barns, for example, may have been built using gorgeous old lumber that can be repurposed. The internet can also be a resource to find repurposed materials. Search listings or create a post for needed materials.

Build an Earthship

The ultimate example of homes made from recycled materials, the earthship was a concept created in the 1970s in New Mexico by architect Michael Reynolds. These off-grid homes are typically horseshoe shaped, feature a passive solar design, and are composed largely of natural materials and common upcycled items.

Reused car tires are filled with compacted earth to form bricks along an earth-bermed northern wall. Colored bottles allow light in, and aluminum cans are placed within mortar walls to save materials. Water is harvested from rain, and energy is generated from the sun or wind. These homes feature many ingenious concepts, although they have their flaws: in many places they do not comply with building codes, and they are not well adapted for locales outside of the Southwest.

ACTIVITY: **Build Your Own
Chicken Coop from DIY Materials**

Owning backyard chickens has soared in popularity in recent years, and for good reason. Many chickens are raised in factory farms and live a very low-quality existence. Raising chickens is a great way to increase your connection to your food supply, source fresh eggs, and have fun. If you have kids, they will likely be thrilled to have egg-laying hens as new pets.

Most chicken keepers use an enclosed coop with a covered area to protect hens from the elements. Coops can be purchased but also can be a relatively accessible building project for someone with basic carpentry skills. A simple coop for a small flock can be built in a weekend.

Whenever possible, build your coop from repurposed materials. Construction dumpsters, stores that carry repurposed building supplies, and builder friends can be great sources of materials. Find a DIY coop design and that fits your yard, flock size, and climate. Online instructional videos can be helpful as well.

Every coop will need nesting boxes, a roosting bar, a feeder, and a water source to provide for happy and healthy hens. As a general rule, you will want at least two to three square feet of space per chicken in the coop and ten square feet per bird in the run. Build one nesting box per three to four hens and include eight to twelve inches worth of roosting perches per bird set roughly eighteen to twenty-four inches off the ground.

Fresh air is crucial; include a vent near the ceiling to remove moist, stale air. This is especially vital during warmer weather when chickens can become heat stressed. Providing some midday shade can also be helpful for keeping hens cool and healthy.

Beware of overcrowding as it can lead to aggressive behavior—provide as much space as possible. Provide bedding and plentiful outside space for chickens to forage and explore. Also, be mindful to construct a coop that keeps out predators, and lock the chickens up securely at night. Even urban areas can be full of dogs, foxes, coyotes, possums, minks, skunks, hawks, owls, raccoons, and rats that can eat the feed, eggs, or even the birds. Keep the feed in a secured container to avoid unwanted attention. A strategic setup for feeding, watering, egg collecting, and cleaning reduces the amount of daily work required.

If you have a clean rainwater collection system, use rain barrel water for the chickens. Supplying artificial light during the winter months, especially in cold climates, can boost cold-weather egg production. Provide additional winter protection and shielding if you live in a cold climate. During the summer, proper ventilation is recommended to prevent overheating.

Once you have an idea of the coop design, put the word out about the building materials you need. Consider repurposing anything from slightly damaged siding and reclaimed barn wood to old shutters and fence posts for your project. Offer free eggs in the future in exchange for building materials.

THREE

ENERGY USE

Conserve Energy

T HE NEED FOR ENERGY IS UNDISPUTABLE, but at what cost? It is essential to seek clean sources of energy and eliminate dependence on fossil fuels to ensure a healthy planet for future generations. As technologies and project implementation advance, there are many ways to do this. Conserve and reduce your home energy use, install renewable energy systems, embrace the full potential of passive solar energy, and stay on top of energy audits and upgrades.

There are many opportunities to conserve energy in your home. Energy-efficient lighting, HVAC systems, appliances, and electronics can save a huge amount of energy—and money. Home insulation, air sealing, and weatherization projects can make your home more comfortable and reduce your use of fossil fuels.

Energy-Saving Habits

There are numerous habits and behaviors you can change to conserve energy. When possible, wash clothes and rinse dishes in cold water and turn off and unplug unused electrical appliances. Heat less in the winter, and cool less in the summer. Using a fan in the summer can make a room feel cooler and lower air-conditioning needs. Replace incandescent light bulbs with efficient LED or fluorescent lights. Run your appliances as efficiently as possible with regular maintenance. Clean your refrigerator coils annually, change the filters on your forced-air furnace and air conditioner, and clean the coils on your window air-conditioning unit.

Even if you rent, you can still try many of the projects in the section to explore ways to conserve resources around the building. Are exterior lights on timers? Do light fixtures contain energy-efficient LED or light bulbs? Are electric-vehicle chargers available to tenants? Are there ways to weatherize the building to lower heating and cooling costs, such as with air sealing or insulating? Are there energy-saving front-loading washers or places to put up clotheslines?

If you have identified ways to green your building, speak with the landlord or management company. They are more likely to be receptive to your ideas if they save money or make the building more appealing to potential tenants. Many resource-saving improvements can also reduce operating costs.

Use Renewable Energy

RENEWABLE ENERGY PRODUCES POWER from sources that are constantly and naturally replenished, such as wind, sunlight, waves, tides, and geothermal energy. Our growing concerns about reducing carbon emissions and air pollution makes using clean energy paramount. It is an easy and obvious way to reduce reliance on fossil fuels.

Go Solar

The use of solar power has surged over the past two decades. Harvesting solar power is clean and versatile, and solar energy is one of the easiest and quickest forms of renewable energy to implement. Solar arrays can be installed on the roofs of houses, businesses, schools, and community buildings in a matter of months. The cost of solar electric installations has fallen dramatically in recent years as they have increased in popularity. Solar panels have up-front costs, but as of 2020, residential solar systems in the United States typically pay for themselves in five to ten years, depending on local energy costs, panel location, and solar incentives. Since solar panels

are designed to last for twenty-five to thirty years, a solar system will produce cost-free energy for many years. With no moving parts, the system requires little to no maintenance though the inverter will at some point need to be replaced.

In 1954, Bell Labs created the first silicon solar cell. Today, solar panels have almost quadrupled in power output, to 22 percent efficiency. Solar panel efficiency gains mean that more power can be generated in a smaller footprint, so many homes can produce all their electricity on-site with the available solar technology.

Finding a good contractor and using quality materials is important for any home-improvement project, and the same is true of solar-energy installation. The North American Board of Certified Energy (NABCEP) has a certification program for solar installers. Certification doesn't guarantee good contractor workmanship, but it does ensure a certain degree of solar-energy knowledge and field experience. If possible, make sure your solar installation is either supervised by a NABCEP-certified professional or that a NABCEP-certified installer is on the job.

Solar Thermal Heating

This technology harnesses energy from the sun for both space and water heating. In residential settings, solar thermal involves installing solar collectors on the roof. Unlike solar electric panels, solar thermal collectors do not generate an electric current. Therefore, some homeowners install both solar thermal and solar electric panels on the same house for different purposes.

As solar electric technology has advanced, solar thermal has decreased in popularity. For example, electric hybrid water heaters combined with a solar electric system are often more economical than installing a solar thermal water heater on most homes. As electric vehicles and heat pumps for heating and cooling grow in popularity, solar electric panels are more attractive because these technologies are powered by electricity.

Join a Community Solar Farm

Community solar farms or solar gardens are a great option in many areas for rentals or homes that aren't suited for solar panels. Members purchase a share or subscribe, for no money down, to an off-site solar farm, where the solar energy is produced.

This model is growing in popularity in states with policies that support these projects, including Florida, New York, Minnesota, Massachusetts, and Colorado. As policies change to support community solar installations, they are likely to become a more available option for solar-energy adoption.

Harness Wind Power

Unlike solar electric systems, wind turbines can generate power twenty-four hours a day, or whenever the wind is blowing. Small-scale wind turbines can be installed on properties to harness wind energy in locations with ample wind resources. Even small turbines require a lot of space, thus they are better suited for rural homes in windy locations.

Large wind turbines are expensive and require a steep up-front investment, but one very large wind turbine can produce enough electricity to power thousands of homes, which makes them useful for powering larger loads like a cluster of homes, a university campus, or an industrial park. For this reason, utility-scale wind turbines are more prevalent and cost-effective than small ones.

Purchase Green Power from Your Utility

About half of all utility companies have an option for residents to buy clean energy, typically for a slightly higher rate. These are often called "green power," "green pricing," or "clean power" programs. These initiatives encourage utilities to install renewable-energy systems through financial incentives.

Although this doesn't offer customers the financial advantages of owning the solar energy system, there are environmental benefits to such programs, which pollute less and don't require fossil fuel extraction. Contact your utility company to find out about the options in your area.

Support Businesses That Use Renewables

We can also support clean energy through our purchases and investments. From socially responsible mutual funds to green purchases and supporting retailers using solar energy, there are many opportunities to participate in renewable-energy projects. Encourage your local schools and government offices to install solar-energy systems to cover their energy needs. As these sources of energy skyrocket in popularity, the chances to support them are growing exponentially.

Encourage Municipal Renewable Energy Use

Many towns and cities are installing solar panels and wind turbines at fire stations, schools, city halls, old landfills, and vacant lots to power their needs. In many places, this is a cost-saving opportunity, resulting in a win-win situation for the environment and the tax-payers. If your town or city government doesn't use renewable energy, encourage them to start.

PROFILE: Smart Living in California

When Andrew Dawn decided to have a new house built for himself and his two children near Sacramento, California, he chose all of the energy-efficient features. Despite very hot summers and 3,100 square feet to cool, the house produces nearly all of its power with a four-kilowatt solar system on the roof.

The house was designed to have solar panels, but the neighborhood association rules limited the size of the array. Dawn is not unique in having a solar-energy system—the majority of the nearby homes also have panels. He also drives a Tesla Model 3, which he charges at work and some-times at home. Dawn marvels at how comfortable the house is due to the tight, energy-efficient construction, triple-pane windows, and generous amounts of insulation. The very low energy bills are an extra bonus

A smart feature of the house is that Dawn is able to monitor his solar-energy production, home energy consump-tion, and electric vehicle using apps. Such systems help identify many issues, such as if there is a problem with the solar energy production or if faulty equipment is wasting electricity.

In the average home, 30 percent of water use is ded-icated to the garden, and mindful irrigation practices can help cut waste. In Dawn's area, the cost of water continues to increase. He uses the RainMachine app connected to the drip-irrigation system in his garden to remotely control and adjust water cycles. This aids in conserving water while promoting garden health. The app—free after a rebate from his city—uses weather data and forecasts to determine the frequency and duration of watering. It allows Dawn to remotely control water use in his garden and provides historical data on water consumption.

"I love the fact that I can see my solar energy production and my utility usage from apps. It's fun and easy to monitor the house, my garden water consumption, and my car. The electric bills are predictable and low, and my house is extremely comfortable."

Passive Solar Heating

T HE NAVAJO PEOPLE OF ARIZONA long used the canyons to heat the southern walls of traditional adobe homes. When the sun is lower in the sky, the canyon walls warm up, slowly releasing heat to the adjacent homes. During the summer, when the sun is higher in the sky, the position of the walls means they avoid the sun's hottest rays.

Properly siting houses involves understanding that buildings are receptors of light and energy. The orientation of a house is one of the most crucial factors in determining how much energy will be required to modulate the temperature. Aim to maximize solar gain when it's useful by siting the house to face the winter sun and minimize it when it's not by protecting it from the summer sun.

Southern Exposure

In the northern hemisphere, a passive-solar house design relies on unobstructed southern exposure. (Siting solar panels on a south-facing roof is also beneficial for maximum electricity production.) When the sun is lower in the sky, it streams in through south-facing windows, warming the home. During the summer, the sun is higher in the sky, and the harsh rays are blocked. Skilled architects know how to properly size south-facing windows to prevent the house from overheating during the spring and fall. Strategically placed window treatments and tall trees and shrubs can also help to maximize solar gains.

Shade Unwanted Sun

Eaves and overhangs help to keep out the high summer sun (and throughout the spring and fall in warmer climates). When properly placed, they will let the sun in when you want it and block it during the warmer times of the year, greatly reducing the need for air conditioning.

Add Thermal Mass

Thermal mass is material that helps capture the sun's heat so it can be used to regulate a building's temperature. Concrete, brick, stone, and tile all absorb heat from the sunlight during the day and slowly release it. This helps moderate indoor temperatures and minimize temperature swings. Whenever possible, allow the sun to hit the floor directly, rather than the carpeting or furniture, so the floor absorbs the solar heat.

MATERIALS with HIGH THERMAL MASS

CONCRETE   BRICK   STONE   TILE

Passive Cooling

A IR CONDITIONERS ARE ONE of the most energy-consuming appliances in most homes. Not surprisingly, space cooling emits significant greenhouse gases globally. One of the best ways to reduce demand for air conditioning is to utilize natural cooling techniques. Passive cooling involves the use of insulation, light-colored exteriors, shading, home orientation, and natural ventilation to save energy while keeping spaces comfortable.

Use Shade Strategically

In addition to strategically orienting homes and window placements, the use of shade can significantly reduce the need for air conditioning. Eaves and awnings deliberately placed, especially over south-facing windows, patios, and porches, are great ways to keep the heat of the sun out of the home. Shade trees and live awnings with vines can be very helpful in keeping homes and yards cool in warm weather. Proper placement is essential to avoid shading out the sun in winter when it is needed to warm the home. If appropriate, deciduous trees can assist in achieving this because most lose their leaves during winter, offering less shade seasonally.

Energy-Saving Roofs

The way the roof is attached can have a big impact on energy performance, so keep energy-saving options in mind when redoing your roof. Shingles that are nailed directly to the roof deck with no air space in between do not perform as well in hotter and colder weather. A batten system is important for allowing proper airflow and also works well with metal roofs. This air space provides insulation and helps to stop the flow of heat into the home during the summer and out of the home during the winter.

Metal roofs have become very popular in recent years. Homeowners appreciate that they last forty to seventy years, making them far more durable than asphalt shingle roofs. They often contain recycled materials and are also recyclable. Solar reflective coatings can be applied to make these roofs cooler during the warmer months. Although the up-front cost is much higher, the lifetime cost is often much lower. If a home has a solar system, there are additional benefits to having a long-lasting roof.

Natural Air Movement

Ventilation is essential for home comfort and indoor air quality. Windows, doors, skylights, and vents can all help bring air in and out of the home when desired. Orienting a home to catch the prevailing breeze is very helpful for passive ventilation. Fans can also aid in directing cooler air into the home.

Embrace the Sun

S OLAR ENERGY IS VAST AND INEXHAUSTIBLE. Each hour, the sun directs more energy onto the Earth than is needed to fulfill its energy needs for an entire year. In addition to using the sun to generate electricity and heat for your home, you can use the sun's rays in all sorts of ways to reduce the amount of energy you consume.

Let Natural Light Shine Indoors

As much as possible, allow natural daylight to illuminate the interior of the home. People are more productive, are less prone to depression, have more restful sleep, build up a stronger immune system, and learn more quickly when they are exposed to daylight indoors.

During the winter, keep the window treatments open to allow as much natural light in as possible. Keep furniture from blocking windows, and use mirrors strategically to reflect natural light. Consider trimming back branches of trees that block daylight or shade solar panels. Spend time in the rooms that receive the most sun.

Grow House Plants

Take advantage of sunny spaces in your home to grow plants. Like daylight, plants help boost our mood and increase productivity. They remove toxins from the air, including formaldehyde (found in particleboard and carpets), benzene (in auto fumes, paint, and glue), and trichloroethylene (in spot remover and paint stripper). Grow herbs in pots on a windowsill to supplement your cooking.

Air-Dry Clothes

In addition to saving energy, this practice also helps prevent stains from setting and extends the life of clothes. Whenever possible, hang your clothes to dry on a clothesline or clothing rack. If you live in an apartment building or in a cold or rainy climate, install a retractable clothesline, use a collapsible drying rack, or hang wet clothing on a door or curtain rod to line dry indoors. Air-drying your clothes comes with the added benefit of providing extra humidity in winter. Place clothes where they can receive direct sunlight or near a fan or heater to speed up the process.

Remove Screens During the Winter

In colder climates during the winter months, remove screens on south- and east-facing windows and wash the windows to boost your solar gains by up to 40 percent. If you have them, use storm windows during the winter. Keep screens installed in the west- and north-facing windows to provide protection from the winter wind, unless this prevents you from using the storm windows. Screens are also helpful in preventing birds from hitting the windows, so reinstall them in the spring.

Insulate Generously

W HEN IT IS COLD OUTSIDE, heat flows from the warm spots of a house to the unheated attic, basement, garage, and to the exterior. When the weather is warm, heat flows in from the outside to the home's interior. Insulation prevents that flow of heat, saving energy and reducing the strain on your heating and cooling system. It saves on energy costs, ensures even temperatures, and helps reduce noise inside the home.

Does Your Home Have Enough Insulation?

One of the best ways to determine if a home has inadequate insulation is by doing a touch test. Interior walls, floors, and ceilings should feel warm and dry. If they feel cold and damp, more insulation is needed. Frozen pipes, uneven home temperatures, and ice dams are other common signs that the insulation is inadequate—often the case in attics.

Air Seal When Insulating

Houses have gaps and cracks that allow unconditioned air to enter. Many people air seal a home by filling up these gaps at the same time they install insulation. Air sealing works like a windbreaker by stopping outdoor air from permeating whereas insulating functions like a sweater. They play an important role in achieving overall comfort and work well in partnership. Air sealing can also help solve moisture issues, which can render insulation less effective.

Stop Drafts

Sealing gaps and cracks around the windows and weather stripping around exterior doors can prevent drafts and reduce your energy use. If you have single-pane windows and live in a colder climate, creating window inserts or installing a layer of clear plastic can result in huge improvements.

Choose Natural Insulation to Protect Indoor Air Quality

Not all insulation materials are natural. When selecting insulation, choose natural options that do not emit volatile organic compounds or contain asbestos and formaldehyde. Avoid products with harmful flame retardants and binders, such as rigid foam. Polyurethane foam is great at reaching cracks and crevices but can off-gas contaminants, creating long-term indoor-air-quality issues. If possible, use Green Guard–certified products.

Cellulose Insulation

This insulation product is blown into ceiling and wall cavities to create a thermal barrier. Cellulose insulation products have some of the best environmental ratings and are made largely of postconsumer recycled paper. The manufacturing of cellulose insulation requires as much as thirty times less than the energy needed to make fiberglass or mineral wool insulation. In addition, because cellulose products do not emit harmful gases, they help promote healthy indoor air. Cellulose is not suitable in projects that require it to come into contact with excessive moisture or water such as in many basements with unmitigated moisture issues. Proper installation is crucial as cellulose insulation can settle over time.

Cotton Insulation

Cotton insulation has many of the same qualities as cellulose and comes in batts and as loose fill. It contains a lot of postconsumer recycled content and is commonly made of recycled denim, so it makes great use of existing materials. The downside is that cotton insulation typically costs more than other products. Like cellulose, it shouldn't be used in places with moisture issues.

Energy Upgrades
and Projects

MANY OF US KNOW OUR HOMES WELL. We can walk to the bathroom in the dark without walking into the walls. We can identify the sources of various noises in our homes, but many of us do not know our homes well from an energy standpoint. In many of our homes, small upgrades and adjustments could save energy, promote air quality, and prevent failure of mechanical systems. Some of these upgrades can be completed easily by a novice, but, depending on your skill level, bigger projects may require a professional.

Conduct a Home Energy Audit

One of the best ways to learn if and how your home is leaking energy is by hiring a home-performance expert to conduct an energy audit. These evaluations typically involve the use of an infrared camera and a blower door test to determine the weak points in the home envelope. They can also help you prioritize home energy upgrades. For example, it might be worthwhile financially to replace inefficient single-pane windows but not double-pane windows.

If you don't want to hire a professional, you can try to conduct your own test. Some home improvement stores will rent out infrared cameras. You can also use a candle to pinpoint smaller leaks around outlets, baseboards, light fixtures, windows, and phone jacks. If the flame dances around, it indicates a nearby air leak. Another method is to listen for a whistling sound on windy days to find improperly installed windows or worn weather stripping.

Maintain Your Heating and Cooling System

Keeping your HVAC system running in peak condition helps prevent high energy bills and the need to replace equipment. Changing your furnace filters, as needed, helps maintain proper airflow, which impacts energy efficiency. If you hear a whistling sound from your furnace, this may be an indication that the filters are dirty. Regular tune-ups for your HVAC system are essential for preventing carbon-monoxide leaks, inspecting the burner and heat exchanger, and ensuring safe operation.

Use a Programmable Thermostat

Programmable thermostats facilitate energy savings by enabling you to preset the optimum temperatures for certain times of the day or specific days of the week. You can save energy without sacrificing comfort by heating or cooling your home less when the home isn't occupied or you are sleeping.

Smart thermostats also allow you to make adjustments from an app or website. For example, if you decide to go out after work or school, you can update the temperature settings around your impromptu plans. Or if you forget to update the temperature settings before going on vacation, you can make these changes remotely.

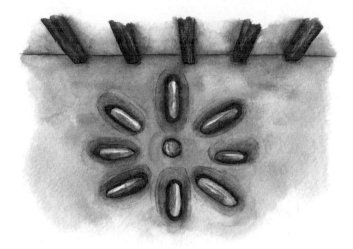

Seal Leaky Ductwork

Leaky ductwork is a common culprit resulting in high energy bills. Gaps in the ductwork allow conditioned air to escape into unconditioned spaces and cause the HVAC system to work harder. The best way to know the condition of your duct system is with a duct leakage test. Unfortunately, ductwork is difficult to access in many houses. Whenever possible, use nontoxic, water-based products.

FOUR

FOOD AND WASTE

A Zero-Waste
Kitchen

F OOD AND WASTE REPRESENT our relationships with our bodies and the world around us. Where they converge is a tremendous opportunity to live in harmony with nature and create balance. Growing, preparing, and preserving food at home, rather than buying prepackaged products, are all ways of reducing waste and dependence on the fossil fuels used in shipping. Composting food waste cycles nutrients back into the earth and also helps to develop a keener awareness of just how much we throw away. Learning how to repair and repurpose household items rather than discarding them, in addition to bartering, trading, and gifting things we no longer need keeps those items out of the waste stream, and also means that fewer new products need to be made. In a material culture, paying attention to everything we consume and discard in our homes is a way to make our lives more sustainable and in alignment with nature.

The average American generates 4.4 pounds of waste every day. Of that, only 1.5 pounds is recycled or composted. This adds up to 167 million pounds of trash disposed of every year across the

United States. There is a vast opportunity to repurpose, reduce, reuse, and, when necessary, recycle much of what is ending up in our landfills.

Because much of our waste originates in the kitchen, let's start there. Striving toward a zero-waste kitchen is a huge leap in the right direction. Take a peek in your trash or compost bin to get an idea of the waste you are generating in your kitchen. Stop purchasing disposable products at the store—this may be inconvenient at first, but it will force you to find sustainable solutions and even save money in the process.

Eliminate Food Waste

To curb the food-waste habit, be mindful of your habits while shopping, especially when purchasing perishable foods, and make smart choices. Consider making a meal plan for the week and buy only the produce needed for each meal. After you make a meal, find creative ways to reinvent leftovers, and organize the refrigerator to prevent foods from getting forgotten. Store food properly to prevent it from spoiling. Keep track of what often gets thrown away and buy less of it or only buy it for immediate consumption.

Compost Kitchen and Yard Scraps

Composting is nature's way of recycling plant matter back into the soil. Food scraps and yard waste make up 20 to 30 percent of the total household trash generated in the United States—starting a compost bin or pile can make a huge difference in diverting waste and promoting soil health. Locate the pile in a relatively dry and shady place.

Feed the compost roughly equal parts of green and brown materials. Green materials consist of fruit or vegetable waste, grass clippings, coffee grounds, and eggshells. Brown materials include branches, straw, twigs, and dead leaves. Keep the materials moist but not soggy and stir your compost once a week.

This simple action can divert a lot of waste from landfills, reduce methane-gas emissions, and help enrich your garden beds. Simply chop your food waste into one-inch segments and stir and water your compost pile weekly. If yard space is limited, an indoor worm bin is an option. If there are backyard chickens nearby, feed them edible food scraps.

Trade Paper Products for Cloth

Instead of using paper towels and napkins, switch to cloth rags, napkins, and sponges. Avoid synthetic fabrics, such as nylon and polyester as they are not absorbent. To save energy, line dry rags whenever possible instead of using the dryer.

Stop Using Disposable Food Packaging

Sandwich bags, plastic wrap, aluminum foil, and wax paper may be convenient, but they produce a lot of waste and are difficult to recycle. Much of the world's shores are littered with plastic. Store food in jars, cloth bags, and reusable food containers rather than in plastic and foil. Also, some foods come in sturdy plastic bags that can be washed and reused multiple times.

Bring Your Own Grocery and Produce Bags

It is easy to go grocery shopping and end up with a small pile of plastic produce and grocery bags. Instead, use cloth bags (you can even make your own out of old sheets or shirts). When grocery shopping, bring reusable produce bags and grocery bags to reduce waste. If you are prone to forgetting, keep a spare one in your car or in your bag or purse. If you don't have them with you and paper bags are not available, ask for empty boxes in the store or market that can be reused to transport your groceries. (Guidelines around using disposable bags have been in flux due to COVID-19; however at the time of publication, many stores had shifted back toward allowing them.)

Shop in Bulk

Many grocery stores have a bulk aisle (also in flux with COVID-19). Bring your own jars, containers, and bottles. Then simply write down the tare weight of the container and fill it up. This is a great way to purchase many common items including dry foods, shampoo, laundry soap, oil, nuts, teas, beans, and coffee.

Make Food from Scratch

Many prepared foods use an excessive amount of packaging. Making these items yourself is a great way to reduce waste, save money, eat healthier, and use local ingredients. Homemade yogurt, ice cream, spreads, salad dressings, crackers, hummus, and cakes are all good candidates. Try out the recipes in the following page and see how much packaging you can eliminate while enjoying tasty treats.

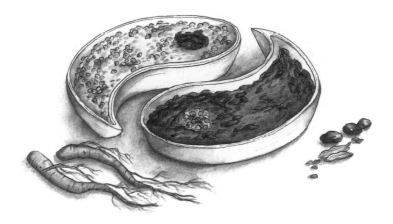

RECIPES: **Make Your Own Nondairy Milk, Salad Dressing, Smoothies, Energy Bars, and Kombucha**

The grocery store is lined with foods wrapped in plastic packaging. The more processed a food is, the more packaging it typically uses. A banana or orange has little if any, a tub of salsa or hummus has more, and a frozen dinner is commonly wrapped in two layers of packaging.

One of the best ways to reduce your plastic waste, save money, and eat more natural foods is to make some staples from scratch. If you are inspired by the idea of rolling up your sleeves in the kitchen, get started with some easy DIY recipes.

Nondairy Milk

Nondairy milk products use nuts, oats, soybeans, or other ingredients and are a great alternative to dairy, especially for people with food intolerances or on a plant-based diet. Most store-bought varieties, however, contain primarily water and a lot of sweeteners—and require a lot of fuel and packaging to transport. But we can easily concoct nondairy milk in our kitchens.

The concept behind making any type of nondairy milk is virtually identical, and the oat milk recipe below can be adapted to different nuts and seeds—try almonds, cashews, hazelnuts, or hemp seeds. Soak raw nuts or seeds in water for eight hours and rinse before getting started.

Oat Milk

This milk recipe makes a great addition to smoothies, cereals, and some baked goods. Experiment with different flavors by adding a handful of berries or cocoa powder.

Ingredients:
- 1 cup rolled oats
- 4 cups water
- 2 pitted dates or 2 tablespoons maple syrup
- 1/2 teaspoon pure vanilla extract

Equipment:
- Blender or food processor (high-speed variety, such as a Vitamix or Blendtec, works best)
- Fine mesh bag or cheesecloth

1. Add all the ingredients to a high-speed blender and mix for 30 to 60 seconds. Do not over blend or it will get slimy. Taste the mixture to determine if you like the flavor and sweetness. Adjust as needed.
2. Place the mesh bag or cheesecloth in a large bowl. Pour the mixture through a nut-milk bag to remove the pulp. Straining is not as necessary for softer nuts and seeds, such as cashews or hemp seeds, because they do not contain a tough outer skin.
   Note: The strained pulp by-product can be mixed into cereal or baked goods for a great crunchy texture.
3. Store in the refrigerator and enjoy it for up to five days.

Simple Oil and Vinegar Dressing

Salad dressing is easy to make and making your own can save money and reduce packaging waste. It also gives you freedom to use healthy oils, such as extra virgin olive oil or avocado oil, and to avoid synthetic preservatives. Most dressings can be stored in your refrigerator for a week or longer.

Ingredients:
- 1/2 cup olive oil
- 1/4 cup balsamic vinegar
- 1 clove peeled garlic, whole
- 1 teaspoon honey
- A couple dashes of salt
- A couple dashes of pepper

Add the ingredients in a glass jar and shake or stir well.

Green Fruit Smoothie

Fruit smoothies are a great way to use locally grown frozen fruit and to enjoy lots of greens. Alter the recipe depending on what is seasonally available where you live. If you want to substitute water for juice, add a couple of dates for sweetness. Unless you have a high-speed blender, presoak the dates in a bit of warm water for half an hour to soften.

Ingredients:
- 1 cup liquid (water, coconut water, juice, or oat milk)
- 1 1/2 cups frozen fruit (berries, cherries, mango, peaches, etc.)
- 1 cup greens (kale, collards, spinach, dandelion greens, Swiss chard)
- 2 pitted dates (optional, especially if using juice or sweetened nut milk)

Place all of the ingredients in the blender until smooth.

No-Bake Energy Bars

No-bake energy bars are a delicious and healthy snack food to have on hand for an extra power boost during the day. No-bake recipes are quick to make. This recipe is easy to alter so try experimenting with different types of nuts or dried fruit. If you want to substitute rolled oats for quick oats, place them in a food processor and pulse briefly to break them up.

→

Ingredients:

- 1 3/4 cups quick oats
- 1 1/3 cups sliced almonds
- 2/3 cup mini dark chocolate chips
- 1 cup natural almond or peanut butter
- 1/2 cup honey
- 1 1/2 teaspoons vanilla extract
- A few dashes of cinnamon (optional)
- A dash of salt (depending on if nut butter is salted)

1. Line an 8 x 9-inch baking dish with parchment paper.
2. In a mixing bowl, combine oats, almonds, chocolate chips, cinnamon, and salt.
3. Measure out the nut butter, honey, and vanilla extract and mix together.
4. Add the wet ingredients to the dried ones and mix until all the oats are covered. Add in a few extra oats if the mixture seems too moist.
5. Spoon the mixture into the baking dish until it evenly covers the bottom. Take the bottom of a jar or drinking glass to press the mixture down and flatten it.
6. Cover and place in the refrigerator for at least one hour. Use a sharp knife to slice the bars.
7. Eat and enjoy or freeze individually wrapped bars to enjoy later.

Kombucha

Kombucha is a sweet and tangy fermented drink containing lots of beneficial live bacteria, B vitamins, and antioxidants. Made from sweetened tea fermented with a kombucha scoby (a symbiotic colony of bacteria and yeast), it's a great little pick-me-up.

Relatively new to the West, this probiotic drink originated in China and has been consumed for more than two thousand years. Kombucha is reported to prevent arthritis, cancer, and other health ailments while promoting healthy digestion. Although sweetened black tea is used to make kombucha, the fermented beverage contains a dramatic one-third to one-half the caffeine content of regular black tea, and, since much of the sugar is consumed during fermentation, it is not overly sweet.

Brewing your own in reusable glass bottles is a great way to reduce packaging waste, save energy, and get creative. Because kombucha is a living food, each batch has its own unique qualities. Making kombucha is quite simple once you get the hang of it, and it's fun to experiment with different flavors and locally sourced ingredients.

Sugar

Sugar is used to feed the fermentation process. It is not recommended to use other sweeteners during the initial fermentation. Use organic, unbleached sugar to ensure that your finished product is as pure and natural as possible.

→

Kombucha Scoby

The scoby, or the "mother," is used in the fermentation process. This leathery, slippery substance is an essential element in brewing kombucha. The kombucha scoby produces a new scoby every batch or two; if you need one, ask a friend who brews kombucha, and pass your extras on. You can also buy them online or through a local kombucha company.

Black and/or Green Tea

Use loose organic black or green tea (less packaging and cheaper) or tea bags. You can use either tea by itself, or blend them.

Ingredients:
- 3 1/2 quarts water
- 1 cup sugar
- 2 tablespoons loose black and/or green tea (4 tablespoons total or 8 tea bags)
- 2 cups kombucha to use as a starter (optional)
- Flavorings (optional): Ginger, fruit juice, dried fruit, honey, and herbs

Equipment:
- 1 gallon jar or 2 two-quart jars (sanitized)
- 1 kombucha scoby for each jar
- Several smaller glass jars (sanitized)
- Breathable jar cover, such as a cloth napkin, coffee filter, dish towel, or paper towel

- Funnel
- Strainer (optional)

1. Make the tea base

Bring the water to a boil and add the sugar. Stir the mixture until the sugar dissolves. Remove the pot from heat and add the tea leaves. If using green tea, let the water cool slightly before adding the tea leaves to the pot. Let the mixture cool until it reaches room temperature.

Once cool, strain the tea leaves and stir in a little kombucha (optional). This makes the mixture more acidic and helps prevent unfriendly bacteria from contaminating the kombucha.

2. Prepare the jars

Pour the tea mixture into the jar(s), leaving a couple of inches of space at the top. With clean hands, add a scoby to each jar. It will likely float on the top but don't worry if it sinks. Using a rubber band to secure it, place a cloth to cover the mouth of the jar to keep out fruit flies and other pests.

3. Fermentation

Keep the jars at room temperature and out of direct sunlight for seven to ten days. You may see bubbles form in the mixture and a film forming on top of the jar. This is normal. Starting on day seven, taste the tea. When your mixture reaches the right balance of sweetness and tartness, it is ready for the next step. It will ferment faster at warmer temperatures, so you may need to make seasonal adjustments to your routine.

→

It is normal for kombucha to have a slight vinegar smell. If it develops a rotten smell, throw away the batch and start over— it was likely contaminated at some point. If there are signs of mold on the scoby, discard it and get a new one.

4. Prepare for Making the Next Batch

Remove the scoby and either store it in the refrigerator or use it for a new batch. If the scoby is getting too thick, you can peel off the top layer. Save a couple of cups of the kombucha as a starter for your next batch.

5. Bottling and Secondary Fermentation

Pour your kombucha into smaller glass bottles, and add any desired flavoring, such as fruit, juice, or herbs. If there are jelly-like strands in your batch, you may want to pour the kombucha through a strainer first to remove them (though they are safe to consume).

Put the top on the jar and store it at room temperature outside of direct sunlight for one to three days. The kombucha should get fizzy during this period. Start refrigerating it once it reaches the chosen level of fizziness, and drink it within a month.

Grow What You Can

MANY FOODS THAT WE EAT travel long distances between processing, packaging, and importing, including food items that may be out of season or more widely produced elsewhere. Growing your own food means reducing the carbon footprint and packaging waste of what you eat. You'll know exactly what has gone into the finished product—from seeds to soil and fertilizer—and if you raise animals, you'll be able to ensure they eat healthy feed and are treated well.

Grow an Herb and Veggie Garden

Healthy soils produce healthy crops. Ensure that your soils have plenty of nutrients, and use organic matter to increase crop productivity and water retention. Whenever possible, direct sow plants to save time over cultivating seedlings indoors, and be sure to plant things in accordance with your local climate. Apply mulch to keep weeds down and maintain soil moisture. If space allows, plant fruit trees and preserve some of the harvests for consumption during colder weather.

If you have space constraints, there is a lot you can do to boost the productivity of small areas. Patios and balconies can be used to grow container plants. Maximize lateral space with trellises allowing plants to climb upward. Consider cultivating plants that can be gradually harvested, like kale, spinach, herbs, tomatoes, cucumbers, peppers, and chard, to ensure you have a steady supply of vegetables throughout the season. Planting two or more crops in succession also allows you to take greater advantage of available space.

Plant kale, spinach, peas, chard, green onions, radishes, and lettuce in early spring as they are relatively cold hardy. Start heat-loving plants, including tomatoes, peppers, cucumbers, green beans, eggplant, squash, and potatoes, in the late spring. Finally, extend the growing season into the fall with a second round of cold-hardy plants.

Forage More

The vast majority of the food we consume comes from cultivated plants and animals. Hunting and fishing are growing in popularity as a way to harvest more of what we eat, find a deeper connection to our foods, and eat like a locavore. Foraging for edibles around the neighborhood is another great way to get outdoors, learn about local plants, and discover some super fresh goodies. Wild berries, greens, teas, medicinal herbs, tree fruits, and mushrooms are often abundant when you know where to look.

Learn to identify plants from an experienced guide, and reference an accurate, up-to-date guidebook to plants in your region. You can discover a variety of methods of identifying plants, including using your sense of touch and smell.

Use caution! Only ever eat a wild plant or mushroom if you are 100 percent sure that it is not poisonous! Also, be sure to harvest sustainably, always leaving 75 percent of a given patch of any wild edible so that it

can regenerate. Avoid areas where many people seem to be harvesting and do not harvest rare or endangered plants. Be sure you are not picking plants that have been treated with hazardous lawn chemicals, and always ask permission before foraging on private land.

Plant a Food Forest

This permaculture approach uses plantings of fruit and nut trees, bushes, shrubs, vines, herbs, and herbaceous perennials to create gardens that mimic a forest ecosystem. Because it uses perennials, a food forest requires less work each year than many garden beds. Once established, food forests can have high yields and provide an exceptional variety of food.

Raise Backyard Chickens...and More

Backyard chickens, ducks, and quail are great for supplying eggs and even meat. They provide chicken manure that can be composted into rich amendments for use in gardens, and also make amusing pets. When selecting a breed, consider whether you want eggs or meat, how soon a specific variety provides food, and what its demeanor and cold tolerance are.

If you can, use nonmedicated and hormone-free feed—ideally also organic and non-GMO. Whenever appropriate, provide chickens with food scraps instead of composting them. Avoid feeding chickens overly salty raw meats or beans, highly processed foods, or spoiled foods. Chickens like to scratch the dirt and explore leaf litter, so provide material to keep your birds entertained.

Check with local regulations before launching a backyard-chicken project. Many urban areas do not allow roosters due to noise concerns, and some limit the total the number of hens per household.

Regardless of local laws, it's important to be aware of the noise levels from the chickens and be considerate of neighbors.

If chickens are not a viable option due to backyard limitations, other fowl may be. Quail are small and can require less space, but they can also fly and need to be contained. There are a few advantages to raising quail. Some varieties begin producing eggs at a young age and need very little space. Unlike with chickens, there are few urban restrictions that apply to quails. They are much quieter and easier to keep in an urban setting. Quail eggs are quite small, roughly one-fifth the size of a chicken egg and are white with brown speckles. Though small, their eggs are delightful and relatively plentiful.

Backyard Rabbits

Rabbits are one of the most sustainable meat choices for urban farmers because they have a very small carbon footprint and are efficient in their calorie intake. They are excellent foragers and produce a healthy, lean meat (although it is much more popular in Europe than in the United States). Rabbits are also happy to help turn kitchen scraps into manure and eat items you may not, such as kale stems and carrot tips

Preserving Food

THE FERMENTATION OF FOOD and beverages has been going on for many thousands of years in numerous parts of the globe. When done successfully, it helps slow bacterial growth and reduces the weight and size of the food, making it easier to transport and store. In arid or semiarid regions, people have long dried food in the sun to preserve it. The Romans and Greeks discovered that fruit could be immersed in honey, introducing jams and jellies, and that this extended the life of the fruit. More recently, humans began using salt to preserve food and since then, the benefits of fermented foods on health have become widely known.

Preserving food is an excellent way to reduce food waste and eat more locally grown foods during winter. As your skills mature, peruse farmers' markets for food you can preserve and store for the winter months. Keep a keen eye out for fresh produce in your home that will soon wilt or spoil and try to preserve it instead.

Use Your Freezer

Your freezer is a powerful tool in preventing food waste. If you cook a big batch of something and realize you will not be able to consume it before it spoils, freeze it while it is still fresh. Cooked food can remain in the freezer for four to six months in an airtight container and still maintain its quality. Although frozen food can be safely consumed after this point, it might begin to lose texture or flavor.

If you have fresh fruits and vegetables that will soon be past their peak, arrange them in a thin layer on a tray and place it in the freezer. Once they have frozen, transfer them to a bag or container. This method helps prevent them from becoming a solid block of frozen food. Frozen fruit is wonderful in smoothies, baked goods, hot cereals, syrups, sauces, ice cream, jam, and yogurt. Frozen vegetables are a wonderful addition to soups, stews, sauces, casseroles, and stir-fries.

FIBER-RICH FOODS for a GUT-FRIENDLY DIET

BANANAS   RASPBERRIES   ASPARAGUS

LEEKS   JERUSALEM ARTICHOKE   WATERMELON

Fermented or Pickled Foods

There are many foods that are absolutely delightful when pickled, such as dilly beans, pickled cucumbers, and carrot kraut. Most pickled foods will last several months in the refrigerator, although please use your best judgment to make sure they are still fresh enough to eat and do not smell rotten. Pickling is a wonderful way to preserve crops from your garden or the farmers' market for the winter. It is also a great way to extend the shelf life of produce that might otherwise spoil.

Firm vegetables, such as carrots, beets, peppers, kale, radishes, cabbage, green beans, cauliflower, cucumbers, turnips, garlic, and onions are all delicious pickled. Wash the veggies well and remove the ends to prepare them. Cutting up large pieces of vegetables helps speed up the pickling process.

Although a variety of approaches exist, most pickling recipes involve vinegar or salt and spices. Some recipes involve blanching the food while others merely involve saturating them in brine.

Mend, Share, and Reinvent

＆

O NE OF THE BEST WAYS to save natural resources is to consume less. Mending, sharing, swapping, and repurposing are great ways to get started.

Question Purchases

Many purchases are made impulsively or because something is on sale. Planning purchases can help reduce needless consumption. Before buying something, ask yourself if it is something you really need and whether it provides significant value. If so, is it possible to buy it used or to perhaps share with another household?

Buy Durable Items

Examine an item for quality, and read product reviews to determine if something is well made. Durable items cost more but need to be replaced less often, reducing waste but also costs in the long run. If an item is disposable, is it made from easily recyclable materials?

Mend, Fix, and Repair

Many items can be fixed instead of discarded, although this is becoming a lost art. Whenever possible, fix or repair items to extend their useful life. Electronics are notoriously difficult to repair, as companies often design them with planned obsolescence in mind. Consider the repairability of an item, as well as whether any batteries it contains are replaceable, and its warranty (for bigger items) before purchasing.

iFixit is a free online community for people seeking repair manuals, parts, tools, and free advice. They rate some electronics based on repairability, making it easier to make informed purchases.

Reinvent, Repurpose, and Upcycle

Allow the phrase "One person's trash is another person's treasure" to inspire you to breathe new life into old things that don't serve a useful purpose to the previous owner. Reinventing objects is a great way to keep valuable materials out of landfills and to add to home decor. Items such as clothing, furniture, decorations, shipping materials, and containers all can be repurposed. Repurpose your Halloween pumpkin into a delicious soup, bread, or pie or use wine corks to make a birdhouse or coasters.

Reinventing items also feels good. We can admire our own ingenuity. It reminds us that we can give things a facelift instead of using up additional natural resources. It helps in creating the cultural shift necessary for a more equitable and sustainable world.

ACTIVITIES: Repurpose Old Clothing and Linens

One of the best ways to reduce our reliance on disposable products and the recycling infrastructure is to repurpose materials to make reusable products. Sewing projects that give new life to old clothing and linens are a great way to get started. The sewing projects here require only the most basic sewing skills and knowledge of the running stitch.

The internet also has a wealth of more involved DIY sewing projects and patterns for repurposing materials, including creating cloth diaper covers or a rag rug from old T-shirts, a door draft stopper from denim jeans, and tablecloths and curtains from old sheets or blankets.

Handkerchief

This simple project uses small squares of soft fabric leftover from another project or cut from a worn-out sheet, shirt, or skirt. You can also use an old button-down dress shirt to make napkins following a very similar approach.

Materials:
- Soft fabric
- Scissors, pins, a sewing needle, and thread
  (or sewing machine)

→

Instructions:

- Determine the desired size of the handkerchief. Cut the fabric one inch taller and wider than the finished product.
- Fold the edge under about 1/4 inch and fold it again so the raw edge is enclosed. If precision is important to you, use an iron and a ruler. Pin the edge as you go.
- Take a needle and thread to make a simple running stitch or use a sewing machine along the edge, incorporating all three layers of fabric.

Sweater Mug Cozy

A coffee sleeve can help insulate either a ceramic mug or a disposable coffee cup. This DIY project makes a great winter gift too! The easiest way to make them is with worn out or mismatched socks although you could also use an old sweater sleeve.

Materials:

- A thick sock
- Scissors, a needle, and thread

Instructions:

- Cut the foot off of the sock, making the top section about a half an inch larger than the desired final product.
- Fold the sock inside out and fold over the cut edge. Sew along the edge. Turn the sock right side out and slip it over the bottom of your mug.

Produce Bag

Turn an old T-shirt into a reusable produce bag so you'll never be without one when you get to the store!

Materials:
- An old T-shirt
- Scissors, needle, thread, and a marker

Instructions:
- Turn the T-shirt inside out and fold the shirt in half.
- Make a cut in an arch shape from a couple inches below the armpit across the chest (removing the neck and arms of the T-shirt). This will become the bottom of the bag.
- Sew along the bottom edge.
- At what will be the top of the bag, use a marker to draw a wide oval, which will become the handle. Cut out the shape through both pieces of fabric.
- Cut horizontal one-inch slits throughout the body of the bag for breathability, staggering them between rows. Don't make them too close, or the bag will rip when filled. Turn the bag right-side out.

Bartering, Trading, and the Gift Economy

꧂

B ARTERING HAS BEEN USED throughout the ages and predates the invention of money. Two parties interested in exchanging goods and services agree to the value of the respective items and make the trade. The value comes from the scarcity of the specific item. You might be delighted to trade your peaches for your neighbor's tomatoes if you have a bumper crop of one and not the other. Likewise, you might be happy to give an hour of time helping someone file their taxes for an hour of gardening help or childcare, trading one skill or service for another.

Bartering is ideal when you have something of value that you don't fully utilize. For example, do you drive your kids to school in a half-empty car each day? Those spare seats may have real value to a neighbor that needs to also get their kid to school, though they have little value to you. Perhaps they can return the favor by providing childcare for a couple of hours on the weekend. Many people aren't accustomed to bartering, so clear communication about expectations is important. Be specific about what you can offer. Can you drive my kids to school each morning? I'm happy to give you a dozen eggs from our hens each week or pick up all the kids after school and drive them home.

Related to bartering is gifting. The gift economy involves giving away goods or services without an expectation of a reward. It is certainly a good way to boost your karma, but it also helps strengthen ties between people. The key is to develop gifting as a common practice within a community in order to keep the gifting cycle going. You may give away eggs to one neighbor, but you can trust that another will share a surplus of vegetables with you, and someone else will offer childcare, and so on. Gifting creates a cycle in which things come back to you but, perhaps, in an unexpected form. It is gaining popularity within certain communities that discourage cash exchange for goods or services.

The coronavirus pandemic has provided some inspiring examples of the gift economy in action as many people have asked themselves how they can help. Friends, neighbors, and families started checking on each other, offering support and supplies, and some communities have formed mutual aid networks. With the shortage of personal protective equipment, people dusted off their sewing machines and got to work making masks, which they often gave away for free. Despite the initial impulse to hoard, sharing became essential. People started giving to others, sometimes with no expectations of compensation, a reminder that our relationships and social bonds provide ways of exchanging goods and services that don't require money.

PROFILE: **Urban Green Living in Chicago**

Looking at the garbage can in Hanh Pham and Joey Feinstein's Chicago home, it is clear that they are serious about waste reduction. The couple is inspired by the Buy Nothing movement, which encourages people to avoid making purchases, instead seeking what they need through "hyper-local gift economies in which the true wealth is the web of connections formed between people who are real-life neighbors." When they know that they will not need something for long, they borrow the item from friends, family, or neighbors. If they no longer use something, they look for a happy new home for it.

The couple has competitions to see how little waste they can generate, and this has shaped their lifestyle. Their pantry is full of items bought in bulk in reusable containers. Paper towels and plastic wrap are nowhere to be found. They have an "eat me first" shelf in the refrigerator to prevent food waste, and the compost bin is used as a last resort for food scraps. They often put plates on top of bowls, which works well for stacking items and eliminating the need for plastic wrap. Pham has even suggested legislation in Illinois to make it legal to bring your own container to refill in the bulk section of grocery stores.

Pham is constantly on the lookout for ways to prevent the creation of waste. She makes many of her own cleaning and personal-care products and puts them in reusable bottles. When dining in restaurants, the couple will bring their own reusable containers for doggy bags, and Pham often encourages restaurant owners to switch to greener alternatives, such as unbleached paper instead of Styrofoam food containers. When they need to buy things, they look for used goods and make purchases from local companies with green practices.

To reduce energy consumption, the couple lives in a walkable community with bike lanes and bus and train routes. Feinstein rides a cargo bike and uses it for loads up to a few hundred pounds. He has biked his son to daycare since he was three months old. The family doesn't own a car and occasionally uses a ride-share service, as needed.

As the daughter of Vietnamese immigrants in a multigenerational household, Pham, from an early age, was taught the value of repairing things to get every bit of life out of an object, whether clothing, hardware, or electronics. Her father was known for being able to fix anything with a coat hanger, and she grew up watching her grandfather make ingenious carpentry creations in his basement workshop.

The couple has been a source of inspiration for green living in Chicago. To highlight the problem of waste, Pham has put on street performances at neighborhood festivals, making dresses out of trash to create beauty from waste. Feinstein inspires youth to take action on climate change as a "raptivist" (rap activist) in school assemblies and has presented to nearly ninety thousand students. The couple has helped secure funding to install thirteen solar energy systems on rooftops of Chicago public schools and has raised $1.3 million for environmental-education and school-based projects. Their vision for a greener world is felt throughout the Chicago area.

FIVE

NURTURING THE LAND

Build Your Relationship
with Nature at Home

O NE OF THE PRIMARY WAYS we interact with the natural world is through our gardens, yards, and patios. This can be a mutually beneficial relationship based on curiosity and camaraderie. Cultivate an intentional connection with the place that you live, whether you are simply recreating outdoors in your yard, observing the local plant and wildlife throughout the seasons, growing native plants to support pollinators, learning about the health of your soil, or growing your own food.

Nature reminds us that we are part of something vast, complex, and ever changing. Unfortunately, as technology occupies more of our time than ever, many people are becoming increasingly detached from the natural world and wildlife. People spend just 7 percent of their lives outdoors, but the physical and psychological benefits of connecting with nature are indisputable. Engaging with the natural world fosters curiosity about and respect and empathy for the world around us.

To build a relationship with the natural world, it is important to be aware of the natural cycles that surround us in our yards and neighborhoods and how those cycles impact our home lives. Using herbal medicines or spending time outdoors simply relaxing or observing, meditating, walking barefoot, gardening, or hiking are all ways of fostering this connection and making the joy of nature a part of daily life. We can then bring this connection with us into our homes.

Embrace the Seasons

Learning to accept and embrace the natural cycles of the seasons and to live in alignment with them can lead to a deeper appreciation of the natural world around us. When we embrace the seasons, we become aware of the changes in our natural rhythms. During the warmer months, when there is more daylight, people tend to spend more hours outdoors. There is an abundance of locally available produce as farms and gardens are in peak production. We tend to socialize more and sleep a little less. During the winter months, when sunlight is less abundant, we naturally spend more time indoors and sleep more. As produce availability changes, adjusting our diets to the season means eating more root crops, apples, squash, and preserved foods and sipping on hot beverages. For many, focus shifts to home life and our internal state.

To deepen your awareness of the seasons where you live, spend time outdoors throughout the year. Observe the changes in your yard or visit a nearby park or walking trail during every season—what animals, insects, and plants do you see depending on the time of the year?

Outdoor Recreation

Many of us have a favorite and a least favorite season, but embracing the benefits of each season is critical to our well-being. Even during the winter, it is important to spend time outdoors and remain active, whether by going for walks on snow-covered paths, trying out skiing or snowshoeing, or studying winter plants and animal tracks. What wildlife can you observe in your garden? What critters are foraging for food or resting? Do you see any tracks? Discovering fun outdoors activities throughout the seasons and connecting with our yards and neighborhoods is beneficial for children and adults alike.

Holidays and Ceremonies

Regardless of your religion, holidays are opportunities for nature-loving traditions. This can be evident in our homes or the gatherings that we host or attend. Easter and Passover dinners are a chance to harvest and serve early spring crops. Memorial Day, the Fourth of July, and Labor Day offer ideal opportunities to gather outdoors with friends and family, go for hikes, stroll around the neighborhood, enjoy the yard, and celebrate the bounty of summer produce. Summer solstice can be celebrated with a barefoot walk, by collecting wild herbs, practicing yoga outdoors, or gazing at the stars. The fasts of Ramadan and Lent give opportunities to be mindful of the food we usually consume. Thanksgiving and the Jewish holiday Sukkot can include feasts of locally cultivated, seasonally available foods and are opportunities to get in touch with gratitude. Listening to the land and actively engaging with nature—for food, leisure, and physical activity—can enhance our bodies, minds, and spirits.

Make Your Garden a Wildlife Haven

AS THE BUILT ENVIRONMENT expands, concrete roads, asphalt rooftops, and manicured yards are slowly replacing patches of swamps, meadows, croplands, and forests. Loss of habitat is causing a decline in plant diversity, and this has a rippling effect on wildlife. As sources of food and shelter decline, so do populations of insects, birds, amphibians, mammals, and reptiles that rely on them.

To counter this effect, create a wildlife haven around your home. By paying attention to your local ecology, observing, and practicing mindfulness around sustainable gardening and landscape practices, your entire yard, garden, or even the balcony can provide food and shelter to a variety of creatures. These actions can expand outward to include creating wildlife habitat in the neighborhood and nearby parks. Creating spaces for plants and animals around our homes connects humans to the natural world and supports and encourages a beautiful slice of life to prosper at your doorstep.

Cultivate an Ecological Aesthetic

The tidy manicured grass lawn has long discouraged gardening practices that provide shelter and food to wildlife. Some ornamental fruit tree species—a part of this trend—have even been bred to produce showy flowers but no fruit. Embracing a broader aesthetic vision that also includes *function* can transform your yard or garden.

Try experimenting with native plants, increasing plant diversity, and avoiding the use of nonnative ornamentals. Choose tree species that are good hosts for local wildlife. Allow patches of native wildflowers to flourish to sustain pollinators. Instead of clearing out all the dead dried-out plants in the fall, leave some to sustain critters when there is little food available in the colder months. Make a brush pile to create a shelter for nesting, resting, and protection from the elements and predators. Avoid areas of bare earth; instead, mulch to keep weeds at bay, retain moisture, and encourage microbes and earthworms. Feed the soil with natural materials, not synthetic pesticides.

Some of these techniques may not fit into the standard vision of a tidy yard, but they will bring a wealth of beauty and wonder in the form of the birds, bees, and other wildlife they will draw in.

Attract and Sustain Wildlife

Planting a garden is an opportunity to attract and provide habitat for songbirds, butterflies, lizards, bats, owls, insects, mammals, and frogs and truly bring a garden to life. Grass-only yards are monocultures that do not support wildlife and also require regular irrigation, mowing, fertilizer, and effort. But if a gardener provides for their needs, wildlife can flourish, even in the middle of a city.

Learning to garden in this way requires attention to the cycles of nature and the life-forms it supports. Seeds, nuts, pollen, nectar, berries, fruits, sap, leaves, and twigs provide food for countless species.

Pollinators—insects, birds, and bats that are responsible for pollinating plant life—in particular, are in rapid decline and in great need of native wildflowers to sustain their numbers. Keep this in mind while weeding, as many so-called weeds—including buttercup, daisies, and even dandelions!—have blooms that provide sustenance and shelter to various creatures. Some gardeners loathe certain trees for being messy (red mulberry and white oak are prime examples), but they provide a nearly endless supply of food and shelter to squirrels, orioles, chipmunks, wild turkeys, quail, and opossum in North America.

Oak trees are exceptional hosts to caterpillars and provide acorns that sustain birds and small mammals. Red cedars create yearlong shelters and nesting areas for birds, berrylike cones for food, and fertile ground for butterflies and moths to lay eggs. Willows provide nectar to pollinators and textured leaves (in the summer) and twigs (in the winter) to grazing animals. In addition, providing water and nesting boxes helps attract and sustain wildlife.

Grow Native Plants

Native plants have coevolved with local flora and fauna, making them essential to the local food web. Native plants support a staggering array of wildlife, from pollinators to large game, but they are often crowded out by invasive or ornamental species, brought to the region at times intentionally and at other times accidentally. In the last five hundred years, in the United States alone, an estimated fifty thousand plants and animals have been introduced, a small percentage with devastating effects.

Native plants are generally far more supportive to local ecology than nonnatives. For instance, native oak trees host more than five hundred species of caterpillars, while ginkgoes, a common landscaping tree imported from Asia, support just five.

Beyond their exceptional value to wildlife, native plants often require less maintenance because they are well adapted to the climate. Many native plants are drought tolerant and have deep root systems. Once established, they can endure periods without rainfall or irrigation. Their extensive roots keep the soil intact and help prevent soil erosion. Natives often require fewer fertilizers and pesticides, preserving water quality.

As you embrace native plants in your garden, do some research on plants that are endemic to your region and that have adapted to the conditions (sunlight, soil type, moisture level) in your yard. Nurseries that specialize in local plants can be a great resource in making your selections. Also consider your intention for your yard: Do you want to promote pollinator habitat, feed birds, produce edibles, or all of the above? Native oaks, willows, birches, maples, and herbaceous plants, such as goldenrod, sunflowers, and milkweed, are great hosts for numerous caterpillar species and provide protein to birds for their breeding season. Serviceberry, cherry, dogwood, spicebush, cedar, and holly provide food and shelter to a variety of birds throughout the seasons.

Support Pollinators

Almost all the world's plants require pollination. A diverse group of species does this essential work, including bees, bats, birds, flies, moths, wasps, butterflies, and beetles. Populations of wild pollinators can have huge impacts on ecosystems and food crops and provide an essential role in food security, but, unfortunately, they have dropped in abundance and diversity across the globe. Habitat loss and fragmentation, diseases, and the use of pesticides are major threats to the existence of these important creatures. There are many ways that we, as gardeners, can help keep our pollen-loving friends happy and healthy.

Native plants are far more appealing to pollinators than introduced plants, so grow pollinator-attracting natives when possible. Cultivate a wide range of plants throughout the growing season, including perennials and annuals with various flower shapes and sizes. Night-blooming flowers, in particular, help nourish moth and bat populations.

Make blooms easy for pollinators to access by placing plants in groups with a variety of flower colors in close proximity. Go wild and provide shelter and hiding places to bees, butterflies, and other pollinators by allowing a hedgerow or the edge of the lawn to grow tall or by leaving a dead tree standing. Although hybrid flowers create the perfect bloom, avoid those created by plant breeders because they commonly lack pollen, fragrance, and nectar, compromising their value to pollinators.

Add a hummingbird feeder to the yard, and create artificial nectar for the feeder by combining four parts water with one part sugar. Don't use artificial sweeteners, fruit juice, or honey. Allow the sugar to dissolve, and let the sweet liquid cool before placing it in a red-colored feeder. Adding a birdbath, water garden, or catch basin for rain can also help thirsty birds and butterflies.

To attract butterflies, try growing plants to feed caterpillars. Keep in mind that some butterflies are only attracted to one or two plant species. Lure monarchs with milkweed and black swallowtails with carrot, dill, parsley, or parsnip.

Provide Supplemental Food

Consistent supplemental feeding throughout the cold months can help sustain birds and small mammals when there is little else available. Fill a birdfeeder with seeds (ideally with a high fat or oil content) to provide abundant energy to jays, finches, cardinals, woodpeckers, and sparrows throughout the winter.

LEARN MORE: Embrace Permaculture Principles

Permaculture is a holistic form of agriculture that works with nature in the local production of materials for food, shelter, and energy while simultaneously regenerating the soil. A radical alternative to modern agriculture, permaculture's principles were developed by Australians Bill Mollison and David Holmgren in the 1970s and are based on a sustainable philosophy of living.

In permaculture, a diverse range of vegetation, wildlife, and animals coexist to create a system that is both ecologically and economically sound. Nothing is depleted and no waste is produced, as everything is cycled back into the system. A well-established permaculture garden takes care of itself and requires very little maintenance.

Common permaculture gardening techniques include companion planting, growing edible perennials, vertical gardening, mulching and no-dig gardening to prevent erosion, worm composting, and catching water in water gardens and rain barrels.

These are the three core tenets of permaculture: care for the earth, care for the people, and return of surplus. From these tenets come twelve design principles to help guide a living partnership between nature and people.

The Twelve Principles of Permaculture

1. Observe and Interact

Discover what the forces and factors are at work on a site by slowing down and paying attention. How do the climate, topography, people, wind, fire, water, vegetation, and wildlife intermingle?

How can we embrace this to create greater abundance for everyone?

2. Catch and Store Energy

Store surplus water, soil nutrients, fuel, and food, restoring balance to the systems we are a part of. This includes using alternative energy systems, such as wind and solar, to capture energy.

3. Obtain a Yield

Before you put energy into something, consider whether it offers a worthwhile result. This applies to gardening as well as the work we do out in the world.

4. Apply Self-Regulation and Accept Feedback

Live simply and consciously, and limit your own consumption. Take personal responsibility for caring for the earth and its people, and accept feedback and learn from mistakes in order to grow over time.

5. Use and Value Renewable Resources

Just as planting an orchard downstream from a forest allows us to take advantage of the water and nutrients that move downhill, the natural systems around us provide value. As you discover these precious elements, appreciate and protect them.

6. Produce No Waste

Waste from one part of our system is feedstock for another. Reuse building materials, greywater, and food waste, and repair or repurpose tools and equipment.

7. Design from Patterns to Details

First study the patterns in your climate, ecology, watershed, and society to understand the big picture. Then use that knowledge to interact with the land in a regenerative way.

→

8. Integrate Rather than Segregate

The more relationships that exist between parts of different systems, the stronger and more resilient those systems are. This involves living in harmony with each other and valuing diversity and differences—both in human relationships and in the garden.

9. Use Small and Slow Solutions

Play the long game by embracing slow design principles. Use local resources that take a larger-system perspective into account.

10. Use and Value Diversity

Variety and diversity are all around us in our gardens, forests, communities, and schools. Embracing this enables us to live in harmony and thrive.

11. Use Edges and Value the Marginal

The importance of edges is often overlooked. Margins are typically the most productive areas of a garden and are the interface between the garden and everything else. Consider the places where water and land meet.

12. Creatively Use and Respond to Change

Considering we live in a changing world, it is essential to creatively adjust. To learn more about permaculture, see *The Introduction to Permaculture* by Bill Mollison.

Nourish Garden Soils

J UST LIKE THE HUMAN GUT is a complex system, garden soils
are a sophisticated system of bacteria, fungi, worms, and other
organisms. A teaspoon of healthy garden soil contains between
one hundred million and one billion bacteria. Microbes cause both
physical and chemical changes in the soil, which releases nutrients
for use by plants.

The soil-food web needs to be in balance for gardens to thrive.
Some microbes decompose organic matter, such as manure and plant
debris. Some sequester nitrogen and other nutrients that are essential
to healthy plants and prevent them from entering the groundwater.
Others make the soil more porous, allowing the proper infiltration of
water and preventing runoff.

Get to Know Your Soil

Sandy soils do not adequately retain moisture and nutrients. Because
they drain well, water and amendments just flow away. Clay soils, on
the other hand, have poor drainage and are so compact that they are
hard to work. Worms are a sign that decomposition is occurring.

Put a handful of soil in your hand and note the texture. Or fill a jar with a mixture of soil, water, and a teaspoon of borax. Once the sediments settle, you will be able to understand the makeup of your soil by looking at layers. Adding organic matter benefits the garden regardless of soil type and is one of the best ways to improve both clay and sandy soil types.

Soil Testing

Knowing your soil can provide insights about what your garden beds need to thrive. Soil tests are a great way to learn about pH levels and the availability of nutrients necessary for plant growth. Look for a testing kit at your local nursery or through a university cooperative-extension program. Check the levels of nitrogen (N), phosphorus (P), potassium (K), calcium (Ca), magnesium (Mg), sulfur (S), and organic matter; also check to see whether lead contamination is an issue.

The three major plant nutrients are N-P-K. N feeds leaf growth and encourages photosynthesis, which promotes lush, green plants. Too much N inhibits fruit and flower production. P promotes healthy fruit and flower development and healthy roots. K promotes general plant health, cold tolerance, and resiliency to disease.

Acidic soils aren't beneficial to many plants. Likewise, low levels of nutrients can stunt plant growth, and too many nutrients can stress plants and pollute waterways. Lead contamination is relatively common in older urban neighborhoods. Knowing your soil can offer guidance about how to make it thrive.

Nourish the Soil

Soils get energy and nutrients from organic matter, commonly from

compost, animal manure, worm castings, mulch, and cover crops, which are often locally available. Composting your fall leaves into leaf mold makes a wonderful soil amendment. Organic matter also helps provide pores for water and air, boosting the soil's ability to retain moisture.

Apply compost from your kitchen scraps, yard waste, or a local garden supplier to your soil. Other popular soil amendments include blood, shellfish, and kelp meals as well as alfalfa, azomite, chicken manure, greensand, gypsum, dolomite lime, rock dust, rock phosphate, and worm castings. Common mulch materials include wood chips, dead leaves, straw, grass clippings, comfrey leaves, and shredded bark. Some gardeners swear by actively aerated compost tea, which they apply to the leaves and plant base. It is loaded with microbes, which can boost nutrient uptake. Others apply urine because it is rich in N.

Avoid the use of chemical pesticides—although they can knock out some common garden pests, they also damage beneficial microbes and pollinators, generating long-term damage. Pesticides also needlessly expose you, your family, pets, waterways, and wildlife to toxic chemicals. Work with nature to control pest populations.

Solarize Garden Beds

Many gardeners place a thin layer of clear plastic with the edges trenched in over moist beds to heat soils up to 120 degrees Fahrenheit. This weakens or kills off soil diseases, weeds, and pests without harming beneficial bacteria and can help restore a healthy balance to the soil's food web. (See page 120 for more information.)

Put the Garden to Bed

In colder climates, prepare your garden for winter. Clear any invasive or diseased plant material and dispose of it. Leave some plants for birds and beneficial insects to overwinter. Cover your garden beds with clippings, leaves, compost, animal manure, and/or other types of mulch to prevent soil erosion and compaction and to replenish the soil after the growing season.

Three Ways to Convert Your Lawn into Garden

IF YOU ARE READY TO CONVERT some or all of your grassy lawn into a flourishing garden, here are some tips for making the change. To plant a productive garden, you'll first need to remove the grass. Avoid using herbicides since they will leave chemical residues. Note that if your lawn has had a lot of foot traffic, the soil might be compacted. Enriching the soil with compost and mulch is a great way to breathe new life into your future garden bed.

Sod Cutting

Using a square shovel, cut the sod into strips and roll it up. This technique requires the most muscle power but can also be the quickest way to remove pesky grass. Once the bare soil is exposed, enrich it. Put down several layers of unbleached paper or six to ten sheets of newspaper. Next, add four to six inches of compost. Then top it off with three to four inches of mulch.

Solarization

If you have time on your hands, solarization—placing clear plastic over the garden bed—uses the power of the sun to bake the grass and any weed seeds. This technique works best during the summer when the sun is the hottest and takes about six to eight weeks. If possible, use repurposed sheets of plastic.

To start, cut the grass as short as possible. Then water the grass to saturate the first foot or two of soil; this allows the solarization process to create steam. Cover the lawn with two-to-four millimeter thick clear plastic. If you need several sheets of plastic, overlap them at the seams. Extend the plastic six to eight inches beyond the edge of the grass because the edges do not heat up as well. Finally, anchor the plastic with wooden planks, rocks, or mounds of soil. Keep the plastic on for a week or two after the grass turns brown. After removing the plastic, cover the area with six to ten layers of newspaper, four to six inches of compost, and three to four inches of mulch.

Sheet Mulching

This technique involves killing the grass by covering it up with cardboard. Start by cutting the grass as short as possible then putting down a layer of cardboard on your lawn with the seams overlapping. Next, put at least four inches of compost on top of the cardboard, followed by mulch. Now you are ready to plant!

It is best to do this during the fall so the cardboard can start to decompose over the winter and spring. Alternately, you can place the cardboard during the spring and cut holes when planting.

Maximize Small Spaces

I T CAN BE DIFFICULT to cultivate food in urban areas. Tall buildings and trees cast shade. Some soils are contaminated from lead. Not everyone has the luxury of a large yard. The good news is that most city dwellers can grow some of their own food and bring a little nature into their lives.

Container Gardens and Raised Beds

Adding containers to balconies, patios, terraces, and paved spaces is a great solution if you lack a yard or if you have contaminated soil. Adequate sunlight is often in short supply in urban areas because of shading, but pots can be moved once or twice a day to soak up as much sunlight as possible.

If there is enough room, raised beds provide space for plant roots to grow down and mitigate drainage issues in compacted soils. Raised beds require piling the soil above the ground surface and containing it in a wood, brick, or stone frame. When constructing a raised bed, be sure to plan on at least a foot of soil, or more if it is built on a paved surface. Raised beds can be densely planted, which helps to

prevent weeds while increasing moisture retention. If soil contamination is an issue, place a liner between the ground and the clean soil.

Encourage Vertical Growth

Another way to overcome space limitations is to encourage plants to grow up trellises, tepees, arbors, and fences. This is a useful technique for flowering vines, cucumbers, tomatoes, gourds, squash, and peas. These vines and trellises can also help provide cool shade to a sitting area, serving multiple purposes.

Interplant and Undersow

Because plants grow to different sizes at different speeds, they can sometimes be planted together in close quarters. For example, radishes are fast growing and will often be ready to harvest before they crowd out a kale plant sown at the same time. Start by determining which plants take the longest to reach maturity. Then select some faster-growing plants to throw in the mix.

Plant High-Yield Crops

You don't see a lot of urban farmers growing corn, melon, or cabbage. There are some crops that work especially well in small spaces and others that don't. Good options for small spaces include tomatoes, squash (grown vertically), peas, leaf lettuce, beets, pole beans, kale, Swiss chard, cucumbers, and peppers.

Grow Fast-Maturing Plants

Choosing the fastest growing crops can allow you to collect multiple harvests from the same space. Many fast-maturing plants are cool-season crops that help take advantage of the spring and fall segments of the growing season. Lettuce, radishes, spinach, bok choy, arugula, and bush beans are very good choices.

PROFILE: Community Foodscapes

Jamie Rosenthal is inspired by the motto "Grow, don't mow." Land in urban areas is scarce and expensive, and many city resources are dedicated to lawn maintenance and ornamental plants at the expense of edible landscapes. Most of the food consumed in urban areas is trucked in from distant places, and few urban landscapes provide wildlife habitat or sustenance.

Rosenthal is working to change that. When he sees a lawn or underutilized public greenspace, he sees an opportunity to cultivate nourishing foods for the local community or to create a small meadow for pollinators. After being a farmer for eight years, Rosenthal dedicated his career to creating urban food forests and foodscapes. He works with local governments to think creatively about urban planning and microfarming and to boost community engagement around cultivating food and maintaining productive landscapes.

Collaborating with city engineers, elected officials, and developers, Rosenthal is working to create new frameworks and opportunities for urban agriculture that enrich communities. He sees foodscapes as assets that help cut through differences in age, income, and culture to build community.

One of Rosenthal's most recent projects is in Clarkston, Georgia, a city known for its multiculturalism and often referred to as the Ellis Island of the South. In collaboration with former mayor Ted Terry and the city council, he was able to launch a dynamic community project. Through his work with the community organization Roots Down, an organization dedicated to urban agriculture, Rosenthal is designing urban foodscapes that are woven into the very fabric of the city infrastructure.

Soon, a micro–food forest with pocket gardens containing pineapples, guavas, figs, pears, herbs, raspberries, and blackberries will provide snacks for passersby. Kids using the bus stop and people walking their dogs can enjoy these refreshing treats. As foodscapes flourish, Rosenthal believes our appreciation for food and the people that cultivate it will too.

SIX

CONSERVING AND PROTECTING WATER

Meter Reader

WATER IS ESSENTIAL TO LIFE. Conserving water and protecting water quality is essential for living in balance with nature. As many parts of the world face droughts, reducing water use and waste is more important than ever. Because of the way water travels, how we use water in and around our homes can greatly affect the health of water in the greater world. Track your water use to identify where you can reduce, install water efficient fixtures and fix leaks, and keep harmful chemicals out of water by disposing of household products properly and avoiding the use of harmful lawn treatments.

In terms of water usage, knowledge is power—do some sleuthing to figure out your water usage and then pinpoint the best ways you can reduce in your home. Your water use affects the planet's water distribution, so conserve! Implement ways to save water. If you receive a water bill, you have a meter. Use the meter and the details included in your bill to make informed decisions about your water use. Be aware that you may not have your own water meter or receive a bill if you live in a multifamily building or use well water.

Most water meters have a display, though some utility companies use a signal to read the water meter. The unit is typically either in front or on the side of the house, near the curb or sidewalk in a concrete box labeled "water," in a water-meter pit with a cast-iron lid, or in your basement (especially in colder climates). Opening the lid to the meter might require a tool, such as pliers or a screwdriver. Water consumption is usually measured in gallons or cubic feet (7.48 gallons = 1 cubic foot).

Reading your water meter can help you determine your total household water use and whether your plumbing system has leaks. Read the meter at the beginning and end of the day to determine your total use, and track your daily water use over the course of a week or month. Once you have this information, you can develop a plan to cut home water use. Compare the numbers before and after you implemented the plan to see if your plan was effective. Keep in mind that home water use varies widely from day to day, based on whether you did a load or two of laundry, watered the garden, or have guests staying with you.

ACTIVITY: Get Low

Conserving water at home requires that everyone in the household be on board with the arrangement. Viewing the house as a whole, instead of as individual plumbing fixtures, enables a holistic approach. Using information from your water meter and the following tips, create a game with your family or your roommates to see how much you can cut your water use at home.

Create a colorful scoreboard, encouraging other members of the household to join you, or to play against friends in other households. Winning strategies include installing low-flow fixtures, using the dishwasher instead of hand-washing dishes, taking showers instead of baths, running only full washing-machine loads, and taking shorter showers. You can also measure the amount of time the shower is run or the number of times the toilet is flushed.

Leak Check

WATER LEAKS HAVE A HUGE IMPACT on total household water use, sometimes without your knowledge! In some cases, adding or replacing a gasket or washer can fix the issue.

If you can access your water meter, don't use the water inside the home for an hour or two. Take a reading at the beginning and end of the time period. If the readings are the same, you either have no leaks or very minor ones. If the second reading is higher than the first, then there's likely a plumbing leak on your hands. Some water bills will also indicate if the water company suspects a leak.

If you don't have your own water meter—for example, if you live in a multifamily building or use well water—you can still do some investigating to try and locate leaks in your home. Does your water heater have water pooling around it? Is the toilet running, or do you hear any dripping or gurgling sounds? Add a couple drops of dye to the tanks in each toilet and wait half an hour. Has the dye entered the toilet bowl? If so, you likely need a new flapper.

Inspect sinks, showerheads, and outside spigots for drips. Keep in mind that sprinklers, irrigation systems, and hoses are also likely culprits. Do you see water pooling or signs of wetness in certain areas of your yard despite no recent rainfall? This can be a sign that there is a leak in the underground water lines.

It's important to identify plumbing leaks and fix them immediately. In some cases, they can also encourage mold growth and even cause durability issues if they cause wood to rot.

Fixture Fixes

T HE PLUMBING FIXTURES IN OUR HOMES—including sinks, showers, toilets, dishwashers, and washing machines—have a significant impact on our total water use. Make a list of all your water-consuming fixtures and appliances. Estimate each device's age, efficiency, and how often you use them.

Water-efficient plumbing fixtures can significantly reduce water use. For example, front-loading washers use one-third the water, energy, and detergent of top-loading machines. A full, energy-efficient dishwasher uses significantly less water than handwashing. When replacing appliances, look for the most water-efficient models.

Retrofitting existing showers, sinks, and toilets can also save water. There are showerheads that use just 1.5 gallons per minute of water, which also saves energy from heating less water. Aerators on sinks can restrict water flow to a mere 0.5 gallons of water per minute. Old, inefficient toilets can use more than 5 gallons of water per flush compared to less than 1 gallon by new water-efficient models. If you live in a rental or are unable to replace a toilet, placing a brick in the tank of the toilet can save water by displacing the amount needed to fill it (as long as the toilet still operates effectively).

Go Grey

G REYWATER SYSTEMS REUSE WATER from sinks, tubs, showers, and washing machines for washing, flushing toilets, and irrigating plants. Alterations to standard plumbing systems are often required to make use of greywater though many states have codes that prohibit this. Changes in policy that promote safe use of greywater will enable the conservation of this precious resource.

We can still make informal use of greywater in various ways. Kits exist that store diverted water from sinks to flush toilets. We can gather water in buckets after bathing to water plants, wash, or mop floors.

Eco-Friendly Flush
(or Not)

MOST TOILETS IN THE UNITED STATES and Europe use water that is clean enough to drink—the average household with four people uses about four hundred gallons of water each day, and toilets use more water in your home than any other plumbing fixture! Low-flush toilets help minimize water waste and offer an easy way to start conserving water. Dual-flush toilets go even further by employing less water to handle liquid than solid waste. The user has a choice of two buttons when flushing the toilet.

The next stage involves waterless urinals and composting toilets that virtually eliminate water and even waste from the equation. Composting toilets use anaerobic bacteria to break down waste to be used as fertilizer—the end product is compost that is safe to handle. Diluted urine can even be used directly in the garden as a fertilizer. Some composting toilet designs are relatively rudimentary; others are somewhat sophisticated (or even luxurious!). Installing one can save thousands of gallons of water each year per person, allows for the reuse of nutrients, can help lower your water bill, and can extend the life of your septic system (also saving you money).

Ditch the Sprinklers

A LTHOUGH SPRINKLERS ARE A GOOD WAY for you or your outdoor plants to cool off on hot days, they are inefficient. Much of the water is lost to evaporation, and wet plant leaves encourage fungus, blights, and molds.

Drip irrigation is a micro-irrigation system that delivers water directly and uniformly to the soil via tubing with holes that release water. This helps prevent water loss from evaporation and water and nutrient loss from runoff by gradually applying water directly to the root zone where it is needed. This technique saves time and water and helps promote healthy soils. It is best to irrigate in the early mornings before dawn for maximum hydration, using a timer to prevent overwatering.

It is also essential to water plants only when necessary. Monitor the soil and the forecast to know when irrigation is needed. Improve your ability to recognize when the garden needs water by noting what the soil feels like when plants show signs of water stress. Grouping thirsty plants together makes it easier to water the key areas of the garden during dry spells. Note that many plants need more water initially and then much less later in the growing season.

Collect Rainwater

T he use of cisterns and terracotta pipes to capture and channel rainwater can be traced back to the Neolithic Age. Farmers needed ways to irrigate crops, especially in dry climates, and large urban areas needed a source of water for drinking.

Today, rain barrels are attached to gutters and downspouts to collect high-quality water for irrigation and washing. Hundreds of gallons of water come off of our roofs during a one-inch rainstorm. Instead of letting downspouts divert water to a stormwater system, installing rain barrels allows the capture of water. The best place to locate barrels is in the shade, on hard ground.

Tap water in the United States and Europe is commonly treated with chlorine as a disinfectant. Fluoride is also commonly added in the United States. Both chlorine and fluoride can be harmful to plants, making rainwater an attractive option for irrigation.

PROFILE: A Yard with a Rain Barrel

When Rebekah and Craig Eastep moved into their Suffolk, Virginia, home in the Chesapeake Bay watershed, they noticed a low spot in their yard where water would pool. The poor drainage often left that section of the yard muddy, making it difficult to use.

A nearby city was offering a very reasonably priced rain-barrel workshop, and they were eager to participate. They brought home a fifty-five-gallon rain barrel, removed the lower section of the downspout, and connected it so that the downspout emptied into the barrel instead of onto the ground. Now, the Easteps use water from the rain barrel instead of tap water, whenever available, to irrigate their suburban yard and small garden. In addition to reducing the water pooling, the family enjoys saving about $20 to $25 per month on water bills during the summer.

Although they live in a neighborhood with a home-owner's association, there were no objections to the rain barrel because it is in the backyard and not visible from the front. They also painted it a bronze color to help complement the landscape. The only issue that the Easteps had with the rain barrel was that it was difficult to use the water when the barrel was placed on the ground. They decided to build a simple brick platform for it, raising it less than a foot off of the ground. This minor adjustment makes it easier to access the spigot with a watering can and boosts the water pressure when using a hose.

The Easteps empty the rain barrel between rain events to help them get the most out of their rainwater-catchment system. This also helps mitigate the drainage issue. In the off-season, they drain the barrel, disconnect it from the downspout, and assemble the missing section of the downspout that they removed when connecting the barrel. It is essential to make sure the barrel is empty during the winter to prevent it from freezing and cracking.

Rain Gardens /
Water Runoff

NOTHER OPTION IS TO DIVERT WATER from down-spouts directly into a garden bed or rain garden. These plantings act like sponges, absorbing the water into the landscape from which it can slowly seep in and spread to surrounding areas, preventing runoff. This also helps recharge the groundwater supply as water seeps down into the water table. Green roofs can help slow the flow of rainwater runoff into the stormwater system, reducing water contamination.

Soils that lack organic matter aren't able to retain moisture well. Adding compost, manure, and leaves helps gardens soak up water. Placing mulch on top of the soil helps prevent runoff and evaporation. Look for locally available organic matter from your kitchen, yard, and neighborhood to use. Some cemeteries have excess leaf mulch, municipalities might make and sell compost, and some landscapers will deliver free wood chips if they remove a tree.

Consider water requirements when introducing new trees, shrubs, and plants into the yard. Native plants are adapted to the local climate and require less maintenance and water than many nonnative plants, especially once they are established. Cater your landscaping to the local climate, placing desert plants in arid areas and thirsty plants in areas of high rainfall (see also page 109).

Also address if there are areas around your home where impervious cement or concrete driveways or sidewalks can be replaced by more porous paving materials that encourage water to drain back into the soil. A temporary approach to this is placing raised-bed gardens on top of pavement.

Keep It Clean

Y OU CAN MAKE CHOICES BOTH INSIDE your home and in your yard that affect water quality far beyond the property boundary. When it rains, water travels over impenetrable surfaces, like roads and concrete, and carries with it oil, road salts, chemicals, lawn fertilizers, and other pollutants. Materials dumped into your drains also make it into waterways. These contaminants are washed into streams and rivers, harming water quality and aquaculture, and causing erosion. Two of the best ways to slow down this destructive pattern is to reduce the quantity of water going into the stormwater system and by feeding it fewer contaminants. You can limit water runoff from your roof and yard by mulching or adding groundcover (see page 115). Whenever possible avoid synthetic pesticides in your lawns and gardens. Nitrogen and phosphorus are commonly used in lawn care, but they can harm aquatic life and cause harmful algal blooms that disrupt wildlife and create toxins. Instead, use natural and organic landscaping practices.

Most nurseries and hardware stores now offer organic options for feeding and treating the landscape, rather than lethal alternatives, such as Round Up, resulting in cleaner water flowing into near and distant waterways. If your plants have an infestation or pest, examine natural options. Some pests can be manually removed, and crushed eggshells can deter snails, slugs, and cutworms. Soapy water, beer, neem oil, garlic, red pepper, or herbal sprays can keep a variety of insects at bay. Identify which pests ail your plants and the best way to naturally respond. Try to steer clear of synthetic fertilizers—when using, apply only what is needed, but avoid doing so if you live in sensitive areas or near water sources as fertilizer applications tend to leach and end up in waterways. Also avoid overwatering plants to stop excess runoff.

Remember that many household cleaners, and automotive and maintenance supplies, contain harmful chemicals. Even when used correctly, these products cause soil, air, and water contamination. Read product labels and reduce or eliminate the use of harmful chemicals. Also, never dispose of leftover products by pouring them out in the yard, down the toilet, down the drain, or into the storm-water system as that sends the contaminants to the natural water system. Rather, for a cleaner and healthier environment, take excess supplies to licensed disposal sites, such as paint stores, auto shops, and refuse centers, to dispose of chemical products properly.

SEVEN

AIR QUALITY

Identify and Avoid Indoor Air Pollutants

لthough it may seem counterintuitive, indoor air is commonly two to five times, or more, polluted than outside air. The U.S. Environmental Protection Agency ranks air pollution as a top threat to human health. Long-term exposure can trigger allergy symptoms, asthma, cancer, and even heart disease. Because most of us spend more than 90 percent of our time indoors, healthy indoor air quality is essential for optimum health.

Common leading pollutants in homes and offices include formaldehyde, synthetic fragrances, particles from cooking, radon, carbon dioxide, and carbon monoxide. Homes without adequate ventilation often have high levels of indoor air pollutants. Ironically, this is often more of a problem in newer, energy efficient buildings that are more thoroughly sealed off.

Promoting healthy home air is an ongoing process that involves being mindful of the objects we bring into our homes, including furniture, cleaning supplies, finishes, air fresheners, flooring, and building supplies. Reading labels and employing certified products that screen for toxins is a great way to start. Ensuring sufficient ventilation helps keep air fresh by diluting contaminated air. House plants can also help clean the air in our homes. Aloe vera, peace lily, rubber plants, snake plant (mother-in-law's tongue), and weeping fig are some of the most effective in reducing indoor contaminants.

We need to stop using toxic products, or at the very least, use them as safely as possible. Fragrances, cleaning products, cooking fumes, shower curtains, and air fresheners are all common sources of indoor air pollution. Check product labels for artificial fragrances, antibiotics, or harsh ingredients. Avoid products that contain phthalates, triclosan, 2-Butoxyethanol, ammonia, chlorine, benzaldehyde, sodium lauryl sulfate, 1,4-dioxane, diethanolamine (DEA), triethanolamine (TEA), PEG compounds, quarternary ammonium compounds, and sodium hydroxide.

If you must use a product that contains harmful ingredients, be sure to follow labels on safe use and proper ventilation. Whenever possible, apply products such as hair spray or finishes outdoors. Keep an eye out for GREENGUARD- and Green Seal–certified finishes and Environmental Working Group–verified personal-care products, which are screened for harmful chemicals.

When finished, safely dispose of unneeded products and avoid keeping them in the home—even storing toxic products can degrade the quality of indoor air. Attached garages are another common source of indoor air pollutants—avoid idling vehicles as some exhaust will leak in to the home. Test combustion appliances, such as gas ovens and propane-fueled stoves, for leaks, and confirm that they are exhausting properly.

Mold and Other Common Contaminants

Biological contaminants, such as bacteria, pet dander, dust mites, and viruses, can also be problematic. Outdoor sources of contaminants, including pollen and smog, often enter indoor spaces. Home air-testing kits analyze indoor air quality while also identifying top issues. For people with allergies, it can be helpful to avoid wall-to-wall carpeting in the home, keep pets out of the bedroom, and vacuum regularly with a high-quality vacuum.

Mold and mildew growth inside the home can also compromise indoor air quality and cause major health issues. It is important to keep home interiors dry and within an ideal humidity range. Inspect for roof and plumbing leaks by looking for wet areas and water stains, and fix any issues right away. Bathrooms can be a common breeding ground for mold and mildew because showering causes the humidity level to spike, especially without proper ventilation.

Reduce Indoor Levels of Carbon Dioxide

Carbon dioxide is a colorless, odorless gas that is a by-product of metabolic activity. Both people and animals exhale carbon dioxide, making it a major indoor air pollutant. When we consider carbon dioxide, most of us think about burning fossil fuels or climate change. Elevated *indoor* levels of carbon dioxide are also deleterious and have harmful effects on the human brain and on overall health.

Many schools, cars, gyms, offices, meeting rooms, and bed-rooms have elevated levels of carbon dioxide that impact cognitive function, mood, and even decision-making abilities. Headaches, impaired mental function, lethargy, and reduced school attendance are all linked to high carbon-dioxide concentrations that many of us are exposed to.

Unventilated bedrooms often have high concentrations of carbon dioxide, especially when there is more than one occupant or pets

also using the room without a sufficient supply of fresh air. Typically, carbon-dioxide levels rise during the night when people are sleeping, hindering restful sleep and optimum health. Keeping your door or windows open or having pets sleep in a different room can help mitigate this. Increasing ventilation and circulation to bring fresh air into living spaces is crucial in creating a healthy home.

Be aware that high carbon-dioxide levels can indicate that other indoor pollutant levels are also elevated because it suggests that a building is not properly ventilated. Carbon-dioxide levels often rise in occupied, confined spaces with tight construction.

Ventilate Your
Living Space

V ENTILATION CONCERNS are most common in newer houses and buildings or spaces that have been retrofitted for energy savings. Fewer air leaks typically mean greater energy efficiency, but this also means less airflow between the interior and exterior. A lack of adequate fresh air in the house can create issues with indoor air quality. An effective ventilation strategy is crucial for ensuring clean indoor air.

This may seem obvious, but it is very important for buildings to have operable windows. If possible, avoid renting or purchasing homes without adequate ventilation. In modern high rises, this is not always an option. In mild climates, window ventilation is handy when the weather is agreeable. European-style tilt windows are attractive because they can help deflect rain and prevent intrusions, making it easier to leave windows open for long periods of time. Regardless of ventilation, reducing sources of indoor pollutants is critical.

In kitchens and bathrooms, exhaust fans and range hoods are effective ways to remove pollutants and excess moisture. However, be aware that exhaust fans can reduce home energy performance when conditioned air is exhausted to the outside. In some cases, exhaust fans vent air inside the home and don't actually remove contaminants. Whenever possible, install exhaust fans that vent to the outside.

Because exhaust fans and range hoods only exhaust air and don't supply it, make-up air must enter through gaps and cracks in the home's exterior to replace the air that was sucked out through the exhaust fan. In some cases, moldy and dusty air from the basement or auto fumes from an attached garage are pulled up into living spaces. Avoid mold growth in the basement, and try to keep musty air from entering the living area by keep the basement door shut.

Heat-Recovery Ventilation Systems

Heat-recovery ventilation systems are gaining popularity as an energy-efficient way to promote home ventilation, especially in colder climates. The heat from the exhaust air is transferred to the intake air, saving energy.

Unlike exhaust fans, heat-recovery ventilators exhaust and supply equal quantities of air, balancing indoor air. The intake air is filtered through the system, removing many common contaminants before it is circulated. The location for the air intake should be strategically located to promote healthy indoor air. In a typical home, fresh air should be supplied to the living spaces and bedrooms and exhausted out of the bathroom and kitchen to remove excess moisture, odors, and cooking fumes.

Design Your Kitchen to Support Clean Air

ALTHOUGH THE KITCHEN IS THE HEART of many homes, it can also be one of the biggest culprits from an air quality perspective, both because of the gas used in stoves and because of smoke and fumes produced during cooking. Explore how your kitchen impacts home air health to get started in boosting indoor air quality.

Home Layout

The layout of the home can significantly impact how air gets distributed within its walls and to the outside. In homes with an open floor plan, contaminants from the kitchen readily degrade the air quality of the living room or other adjoining spaces. In apartments, kitchens are often smaller and have fewer windows, obstructing circulation. In older housing, ventilation systems may not exist or may not properly vent contaminants out of the home. When possible, install and use a range hood that vents kitchen air to the outside and have a layout that keeps kitchen fumes outside of the living areas. If these are not options, using a window fan can help remove contaminants.

Stoves and Ovens

Cooking with propane and natural gas can emit carbon dioxide, carbon monoxide, nitrogen dioxide, formaldehyde, and particulates. Electric stoves can also emit high levels of particulates into the air but typically produce fewer contaminants overall. Regardless of your cooking fuel, be diligent about keeping the burners and oven clean. When drips occur, clean them up quickly.

Kitchen Ventilation

Although exhausting conditioned air isn't good from an energy-efficiency standpoint, it does help improve indoor air quality. Whenever possible, use a high-efficiency range hood and keep it on the highest setting while cooking. Ideally, the range hood is located over the stove and has vertical side shields. Make sure to clean the grease traps regularly.

Unfortunately, many exhaust fans, especially in older homes, do not vent to the outside and merely recirculate the air within the kitchen. Examine your range hood to determine if the ductwork runs to the outdoors. If you don't have a range hood, open the windows for ventilation when you cook.

When buying a new range hood, find one that covers the entire stove. Look for a range hood that moves at least two hundred cubic feet of air per minute and is certified by the Home Ventilating Institute. Choose a model that operates quietly, so you are more likely to use it.

Self-Cleaning Oven Cycles

Running the self-cleaning cycle on the oven releases a lot of contaminants, including carbon monoxide, as food debris burns away.

If possible, clean the oven with soap instead. If you do run the self-cleaning cycle, ensure that the home is unoccupied and generously ventilate the kitchen. Bring pets outdoors or far away from the kitchen to a well-ventilated area.

Nonstick Cookware

Nonstick cookware, including brands like Teflon, contains a coating of polytetrafluoroethylene, or PTFE, which makes pots and pans easy to clean. Unfortunately, the PTFE coating will eventually degrade and can produce harmful fumes when heated, especially at high temperatures. Inhaling these fumes can produce flu-like symptoms. Although there are new nonstick alternatives, they are also expected to have similar toxicity.

If using nonstick pans, do not preheat them, cook at high temperatures, or put them in the dishwasher. Better yet, find natural alternatives, such as cast iron and carbon steel. Season these pans with oil to create a natural nonstick coating.

Reduce
Off-Gassing

I T IS ESSENTIAL TO BE MINDFUL OF what substances we bring into our homes and the impact those can have on our health. If you are installing a new rug, cabinets, or insulation or remodeling your home, look for the cleanest products available on the market that don't off-gas toxins into the air. The ultimate effects of many chemicals used in manufacturing today are unknown. Some chemicals are suspected or known to be unsafe at certain levels, of which volatile organic compounds (VOCs) are an example. VOCs are emitted into the air as contaminants, and are commonly found in furniture, carpeting, engineered wood products, finishes, and insulation. Also, look for organic cotton, hemp, bamboo, wool, and wood products in rugs, mattresses, and sofas that aren't treated with harmful flame retardants or finishes.

Contaminants in Home Building and Renovations

If you are doing a home-renovation project, it can be difficult to use only natural products. If you can't avoid using something that off-gasses chemicals, ventilate the home as much as possible to dilute contaminants, and complete renovations during a season when the windows can be left open.

If you are building a new home, avoid insulation made with synthetic materials, chemical flame retardants, asbestos, and formaldehyde. Use GREENGUARD-certified products made from recycled cellulose or cotton, when possible. Certain types of spray foam insulation are known to off-gas, so use these products as sparingly as possible.

Delay Bringing New Products Indoors

If you have just purchased new cabinets, carpeting, or furniture, unwrap and leave them in the garage for several days if possible, especially if the items have been treated with flame retardants or other chemical finishes.

Nontoxic
Home Furnishings

MANY MAINSTREAM mattresses, sofas, and pillows contain petroleum-based ingredients and toxic brews of
chemicals, including mercury, flame-retardant chemicals, and formaldehyde. Because most of us spend hours a day in
an enclosed space while sleeping, the chemicals off-gassing from
mattresses and pillows can be particularly harmful to our health.
When prioritizing natural-furniture purchases, start with pillows and
mattresses.

In addition to comfort, when purchasing home furnishings, consider these questions: Where were the materials sourced? Do the beds
or pillows contain petroleum-based products? Are they treated with
harmful flame retardants?

Federal regulations require mattresses to be flame resistant, but
most manufacturers use controversial chemicals because they are
more cost-effective than natural options. There are natural flame
retardants that meet fire-resistant guidelines, such as hydrated silica,
natural thistle, and wool.

When shopping for a new pillow, mattress, or sofa, look for brands that feature certified organic natural latex, cotton, or wool, and are GREENGUARD and CertiPUR-US certified. Support companies that offset carbon emissions from shipping and participate in charitable giving programs.

Several green mattress and bedding companies have risen to the challenge of manufacturing clean, earth-friendly products. Some of the best green-pillow companies currently include Avocado, Holy Lamb Organics, Naturepedic, PlushBeds, and White Lotus. Avocado, Brentwood Home, Naturepedic, and Saatva are leaders in sustainable mattresses. Many of these models are available only online.

Some green-mattress manufacturers will even take your old one for recycling when they deliver the new one. Otherwise, mattress-recycling options vary widely by location. Another eco-friendly way to dispose of your old mattress is to donate it or give it away for free. Because of the contents and size of mattresses, avoid disposing of them in a landfill.

ACTIVITY: Make Your Own Nontoxic Cleaning Products

Cleansing our homes is a routine part of life. It helps create healthy, sanitary, and pleasant living environments. Unfortunately, many store-bought cleaning products contain toxins, including synthetic fragrances and volatile organic compounds, that are harmful to our health and that can cause respiratory issues, allergic reactions, headaches, or even cancer.

Thankfully, it isn't necessary to pollute our homes to sanitize. The best way to find truly healthy and natural cleaning products is to seek out GREENGUARD and Green Seal–certified products or to make your own. With a few basic ingredients, it is easy to make a variety of cleaning products. Baking soda, washing soda, white vinegar, hydrogen peroxide, Castile soap, borax, and essential oils are staple ingredients in many recipes. Reuse spray bottles and jars to reduce waste, and buy ingredients in bulk when possible.

Note: The coronavirus pandemic has caused escalated concern about disinfecting surfaces. Hydrogen peroxide, when used properly, is effective against coronaviruses and a suitable alternative to bleach and alcohol.

Natural Disinfectant

This method is a great way to disinfect a variety of hard surfaces, including counters, sinks, vanities, doorknobs, light switches, and cutting boards. Hydrogen peroxide, in particular, is known for its powerful bactericidal and virucidal properties. When combined with vinegar, the two form a powerful team. Begin by cleaning surfaces with soap or an all-purpose cleaner before sanitizing.

Keep in mind that hydrogen peroxide breaks down in the light so store it in a dark bottle or in a dark place. Also, it can have bleaching properties, so be careful when using it on fabrics and soft surfaces.

Materials:
- 3% hydrogen peroxide
- White vinegar
- Two spray bottles (any size)
→

Instructions:

- Fill one spray bottle with hydrogen peroxide. Fill a separate spray bottle with white vinegar. *Do not combine the two ingredients before applying.*
- Spray a couple times from each bottle onto a surface. Let stand for several minutes before wiping off or leave it to dry naturally.

All-Purpose Surface Cleaner

This product is very versatile and effective in cleaning many different areas of the home. Vinegar is tough on grease and mineral deposits. Experiment with different combinations of essential oils to find a scent that you enjoy.

Materials:

- 1 cup white vinegar
- 1 cup water
- 1/2 teaspoon liquid dish soap
- 30 drops lemon essential oil
- 20 drops other essential oils

Instructions:

- Combine all the ingredients and mix. Add the mixture to a spray bottle, and store it out of direct sunlight.

Natural Laundry Detergent

This simple recipe is effective for cleaning clothes in both a standard or high-efficiency washing machine. Add several drops of your favorite essential oils to add a gentle, natural fragrance, or make an unscented product by using fragrance-free bar soap without any essential oils. Use one to two tablespoons of the detergent per load, more for a standard washing machine.

Materials:
- 1 cup washing soda
- 1 cup borax
- 1 bar of soap (Fels-Naptha and Castile soap are good options)
- A few drops of essential oils (optional)
- Metal grater or food processor
- Bowl
- Jar with lid for storage

Instructions:
- Finely grate one bar of soap.
- Place the grated bar soap, washing soda, borax, and essential oils in a bowl and mix.
- Store all the ingredients in a jar.

Laundry Stain Remover

Effectively removing stains from clothes is a great way to extend their life. The dish soap helps break down oil and the peroxide causes stains to fade or disappear. Be aware that peroxide can have a lightening effect, so exercise caution when applying it to colored clothes. Treat the stain by applying the stain remover an hour or two before laundering and then working it into the fabric.

Experiment with different recipes and combinations of essential oils to find your favorite cleaning properties and scents. Once you have some staple ingredients in the home, it is easy to whip up a new batch.

Materials:
- 1/2 cup hydrogen peroxide
- 1/4 cup liquid dish soap
- A couple teaspoons baking soda (optional)

Instructions:
- Mix the ingredients together and store in a dark bottle.

Essential Oils for Relaxation, Health, and Cleaning

Essential oils are extracted from plants and come in a concentrated liquid form. Each has different qualities depending on the originating plant. Some oils, such as lavender and ylang-ylang, have calming effects and promote relaxation and mental clarity. Others, such as tea tree, peppermint, and lemon oils, have antiseptic properties and are effective against certain viruses. Look for essential oils with the qualities you desire to make customized formulas for your home, whether to use in cleaning supplies, skin products, or diffusers.

Aromatherapy

Although we now rely less on our sense of smell for survival than we have in the past, scents still have an incredibly powerful effect on our moods, memories, health, and overall well-being. Essential oils intentionally stimulate areas of our limbic system to alter our emotions and behavior. Aromatherapy has been used throughout the ages to promote health and well-being and to lower blood pressure, prevent panic attacks, and ease tense muscles. Essential oils also provide a healthier and safer alternative to artificially scented candles and air fresheners.

Lavender is excellent for relaxation and calming and is effective in treating a variety of health ailments. Frankincense has been used since Biblical times as an antidepressant and to relieve stress, anxiety, and anger. Orange oil is known for uplifting the spirit and for treating anxiety, depression, and nervous disorders. With a history of use throughout Asia, ylang-ylang is known to treat depression, insomnia, and stress and to treat wounds.

The best way to select essential oils for the first time is in a store with testers. Smell them and pay attention to the response in your body. Identify some of the most relaxing oils and blends. Essential oils can be used individually or you can even create blends of your favorite oils. Take care not to use essential oils on or around pets without researching and talking to your vet as many are toxic to animals, especially to cats.

A diffuser is a simple and easy vessel for using essential oils around the home or office. Drops of oils are also great to add to the bath or put on your pillow at night.

RESOURCES

ONLINE RESOURCES

Chapter 1: Establishing Your Humane Home

—

"10 Best Credit Unions of 2020,"
Nerdwallet
   www.nerdwallet.com/blog/banking/
   best-credit-unions
American Tiny House Association
   www.americantinyhouseassociation.org
Buy Nothing Project
   www.buynothingproject.org
CohoUS: A Community of Communities
   www.cohousing.org
Decluttr
   www.decluttr.com
Ecovillage Ithaca
   www.ecovillageithaca.org
The Environmental Protection Agency
   (EPA) Green Vehicle Guide
   www.epa.gov/greenvehicles
Foundation for Intentional Community
   www.ic.org

Chapter 2: Sustainable Building Materials and Techniques

—

Buildsite
   www.buildsite.com
Cobb Cottage Company
   www.cobcottage.com
Greenfiber
   www.greenfiber.com
Green Seal Certification
   www.greenseal.org
Habitat for Humanity ReStores
   www.habitat.org/restores
Old House Online (architectural salvage)
   www.oldhouseonline.
   com/interiors-and-decor/
   where-to-shop-for-architectural-salvage
PHIUS (Passive House Institute US, Inc.)
   www.phius.org

Chapter 3: Energy Use

—

"Buying Clean Electricity," Energy.gov
www.energy.gov/energysaver/
buying-and-making-electricity/
buying-clean-electricity
Energy Sage, Home Solar Energy Quotes
www.energysage.com
"Passive Solar Home Design," Energy.gov
www.energy.gov/energysaver/
energy-efficient-home-design/
passive-solar-home-design
"The Secret to Programming Your
Thermostat the Right Way for Each Season,"
Houselogic
www.houselogic.com/save-money-
add-value/save-on-utilities/
programmable-thermostats
"Small Wind Electric Systems," Energy.gov
www.energy.gov/energysaver/
save-electricity-and-fuel/
buying-and-making-electricity/
small-wind-electric-systems

Chapter 4: Food and Waste

—

"10 Compost Bin Plans," The Spruce
www.thespruce.com/
compost-bin-plans-4769337
"Composting At Home,"
Earth 911 Recycling Guide
www.earth911.com/
recycling-center-search-guides/
The Environmental Protection Agency (EPA)
www.epa.gov/recycle/composting-home
Food Huggers
foodhuggers.com

The Forest Feast (website and
cookbook series)
www.theforestfeast.com
"How To Make Kombucha Tea at Home,"
iFixit: The Free Repair Manual
www.ifixit.com
The Kitchn
www.thekitchn.com/how-to-make-
kombucha-tea-at-home-cooking-lessons-
from-the-kitchn-173858
Local Harvest: Farmers' Market and
CSA Farm Database
www.localharvest.org
Skoy Sustainable Cleaning Products
www.skoycloth.com
Stasher Nontoxic Food Storage
www.stasherbag.com

Chapter 5: Nurturing the Land

—

"13 DIY Bird Feeders," Country Living
www.countryliving.com/diy-crafts/
how-to/g3060/diy-bird-feeders
Audubon Native Plants Database
www.audubon.org/native-plants
Community Foodscapes, Atlanta, Georgia
www.communityfoodscapes.org
Permaculture Research Institute
www.permaculturenews.org
Pollinator Partnership
www.pollinator.org
"Vegetable Container Gardening
for Beginners," The Spruce
www.thespruce.com/vegetable-container-
gardening-for-beginners-848161

Chapter 6: Conserving and Protecting Water

—

The Environmental Protection Agency (EPA) Guide to Rain Barrels
www.epa.gov/soakuptherain/
soak-rain-rain-barrels

The Environmental Protection Agency (EPA): Water Sense
www.epa.gov/watersense/start-saving

Gardens Alive
www.gardensalive.com

Greywater Action
www.greywateraction.org

The Water Project
www.thewaterproject.org

Chapter 7: Air Quality

—

Avocado Organic Mattresses
www.avocadogreenmattress.com

Grove Collaborative
www.grove.co/home

Holy Lamb Organics
www.holylamborganics.com

Naturepedic Organic Mattresses
www.naturepedic.com

PlushBeds
www.plushbeds.com

FURTHER READING

Angier, Bradford. *How to Eat in the Woods: A Complete Guide to Foraging, Trapping, Fishing, and Finding Sustenance in the Wild*. Black Dog & Levanthal, 2016.

Lawson, Nancy. *The Humane Gardener: Nurturing a Backyard Habitat for Wildlife*. Princeton Architectural Press, 2017.

Mollison, Bill. *Introduction to Permaculture, Rev. ed*. Ten Speed Press, 1997.

Schneider, Angi. *The Ultimate Guide to Preserving Vegetables: Canning, Pickling, Fermenting, Dehydrating and Freezing Your Favorite Fresh Produce*. Page Street Publishing, 2020.

Acknowledgments

This book was written from a place of inspiration and wonder at the world around us. There are many people who inspired and encouraged me along the way. My parents, Mary Ann and David Feinstein, helped teach me about the importance of conserving resources at a young age and nurtured my love for nature. Joey Feinstein and Hanh Pham work tirelessly to inspire youth as sustainability leaders and raise the bar on home waste reduction efforts. My neighbors at Belfast Cohousing & Ecovillage accepted my family with open arms, making it simple to live in a net-zero home with an on-site CSA farm. Jennifer Tobin and Bill Smith encouraged me to get a backyard flock of laying hens that quickly became pets. Countless friends have nudged me to write a book for years until Jan Hartman reached out with the vision for this book, and it has finally become a reality.

Contributors

Sarah Lozanova is a sustainability consultant, environmental journalist, and copywriter. Her writing appears in *Mother Earth Living*, *Green Builder*, *Solar Today*, *Home Power*, *Windpower Engineering & Development*, and *Green Business Quarterly*. She teaches courses in environmental business at Unity College and lives at Belfast Cohousing & Ecovillage in midcoast Maine.

Candace Rose Rardon is a travel writer, illustrator, and visual storyteller. Her artwork has appeared in places such as *National Geographic*, *Longreads*, and *BBC Travel*, and she's also a Sleep Story writer for the popular meditation app Calm. Originally from Virginia, she is now based in Montevideo, Uruguay.